FROM
THE
ASHES

ASHLEY CHESNEY

To contact the author to speak at your event, visit:
www.ashleychesney.org

Cover Design by Amy Miller
Interior Design by www.BookBloks.com
Cover Photography by Donna Jean Photography | www.donnajean.photography

Paperback ISBN: 978-1-7350882-8-0
eBook ISBN: 978-1-7350882-9-7

Printed in the United States of America
20 19 18 17 16 15 14 13 12 11 10 9 8 7 6 5 4 3 2

First Edition

TABLE OF CONTENTS

For all the girls still waiting to experience their rising,
this is for you.

INTRODUCTION

While in "the life" and at the beginning of my incarceration, I never thought, *This is going to turn out great in the end.*

I never thought about God or that He gives His best to us. I didn't know that when things that happen in the dark get exposed, He turns them around for His glory. I never thought, *Oh, I'm going through this now because God has something better for me.*

Yet that is exactly what happened.

Mary DeMuth says, "My slavery led to my emancipation," and I agree. I was trafficked and a slave to sex, a slave to drugs, and a slave to the darkness. But when I arrived in a jail cell, that was actually the beginning of my freedom. I was a prisoner—but I was no longer "imprisoned." God redeemed my life from the pit.

The story you hold in your hands is redemptive. God orchestrated it that way, and I wrote it to be a tool for understanding—a snapshot into a life you may have never otherwise encountered. Maybe you are a service provider, a curious individual, or a survivor yourself. Whoever you are, I pray this book instills hope and allows you to show compassion to the next woman or girl you meet on your life's journey. We all have a story waiting to be discovered.

The subject matter in this book is heavy and raw and may trigger certain readers, yet this book will help you help others. It uncovers some of the tactics and recruitment techniques abusers, traffickers, and perpetrators use on their victims. You will also gain better insight and understanding of trauma and the lasting impact it has on the brain and body. You will witness the relentless pursuit of drug abuse and addiction—but also I hope you see the glaring evidence of God. He does His best work as He exposes what is in the dark, and His best work looks like redeeming lives and setting captives free.

CHAPTER 1

Therefore I am now going to allure her;
I will lead her into the wilderness
and speak tenderly to her.

—HOSEA 2:14 (NIV)

When I got out of prison, I felt like my life truly began. Much of my life before that day can be described only in chunks. Pieces of fragmented memory, not properly assembled. Things I was able to remember only as I began to heal.

As a teenager, I would walk home from school and typically arrive at an empty house, where I ate chocolate chips by the handful with *Degrassi* on in the background and dragged a knife across my forearm. I remember the blade being dull; I didn't choose the right tool, but after carving for a while, it temporarily numbed and I liked that. Eventually I got smart and began using razor blades stolen from my dad's garage. The fine line, the precision, the blood drawing quickly. Painless at first, then a sharp stinging sensation again followed by pleasant and satisfying numbness, giving me the relief I was subconsciously chasing. Numbing my insides as my outsides bled.

I was thirteen years old, and this was my attempt at coping. My attempt at dealing with the unbearable physical pain my body felt as my emotions betrayed me. I didn't know what was going on; my brain blocked out an event at the age of ten to protect me, but my body remembered. The human brain was created with intricate protective mechanisms, and my brain did its job. It held on to that memory so tightly, afraid the rest of me would see it—hiding it, burying it deep in my flesh. For reasons I could not tell you at the time, I felt this need for release, to feel alive, to cope with overwhelming emotions. So I cut.

To be clear, I came from a loving home. My good-natured parents encouraged and supported me, and my brother and I did not want for anything. I played sports, received top grades, and had lots of friends. Our home was a place where everyone hung out, and we had the latest gadgets and toys. Privilege rang stale in the air. I say this because I believe it is a common misconception that the dangerous life I encountered as a young adult happens only to children from impoverished broken homes, foster kids, or youth otherwise labeled "at risk." That was not my story. I was essentially the girl next door, yet a secret lay trapped inside me. Since my brain protected me from it, my behavior told the story—a story my parents could not understand.

***

Over the years, I spent *many* nights at a friend's house. I was around ten years old when her older brother molested me. His room had a better TV or some kind of cool electronic setup that we were never allowed access to. But on this particular night, he let us in.

The movie played, the soft glow from the screen the only light in the room. He adjusted his seat, changing his vantage point, and then silently got up and lay down behind me on the futon sofa.

Wait, I thought, not understanding. *Why is he so close?*

Before that moment, I was just the friend of his annoying little sister. She and I were the reason NO GIRLS ALLOWED signs existed. But something had shifted.

I lay very still. He began touching me in a way nobody had ever touched me. He ground himself up and down behind me until, I'm assuming, he finished. I remember feeling confused because this person was supposed to be *safe* for me. But I also felt desired—for the first time in my life.

This memory resurfaced when I was twenty-two years old. For twelve years, my body held this secret. I don't mean to excuse any of my subsequent actions as an adolescent, but *this* finally gave an answer for many of my unexplainable behaviors.

My parents questioned my mood swings and the acting out, and when they saw what I was doing to my arms, they were truly confused. To them, this just didn't add up. I had a great life—what could possibly warrant self-mutilation? I didn't have an answer for them at the time.

I didn't know what was wrong with me. Only that I felt trapped inside my body, and I looked for any way to change how I felt. I began to feel an attraction to the darkness. I don't know if I *always* had it or if it came after the abuse, but I read books about drugs before I ever did them. Ellen Hopkins' stories of girls who came from trailer parks and abusive stepfathers—I immersed myself in these stories, which is odd, considering how my life panned out.

I learned that cutting, experimenting with drugs and alcohol, and—eventually—sex changed the way I felt inside. Seeking validation became an addiction in itself. Sex was tarnished the moment I found out what it was; I now saw it as a tool. Sex was what men wanted, and they took it—at a woman's expense. Sex meant somebody desired you. I didn't see it as a mutual exchange, only something to please another person, to "make them happy." This warped view of sexuality contributed to my promiscuous behavior from my young teen years into my early twenties.

***

My very best friend, Sienna, lived just a few streets down from me. I spent the night at her house most weekends. She was one of those friends who was warm and comforting, and she felt like home. She was shelter from the cold, like liquid light, and I loved being around her. I also envied the way she embodied freedom. She was confident, funny, and didn't seem to have all the insecurities I felt as a young teen.

During the summer between seventh and eighth grade, I began realizing for the first time that I could change the way I felt. The constant gnawing in the pit of my stomach went away with alcohol. One particular night, we—Sienna, another friend of ours, and I—made a plan: We were going to get drunk for the first time and "camp" in Sienna's front yard in a one-person tent. Great idea. My dad was in the restaurant industry, and we had cupboards full of alcohol. I dumped out a water bottle and filled it back up with a teeny, tiny bit of every kind of alcohol I could find, plus a Heineken. My other friends contributed a total of one can of Bud Light, or something of that nature, and we were golden.

I blacked out the first time I drank. In my defense, I believe anybody who drank that concoction we made would've blacked out, but nonetheless, this set the tone for my drinking later on.

Everything was giant in Sienna's house. I loved that house, with the giant front door, the giant door knocker, giant couches that wrapped around you like a hug as you sank into them, and—of course—the giant concrete steps that I decided to do a "trust fall" off of. As the other girls giggled inside the tent, I fell backward off the steps. The next morning, nursing my first hangover and the cuts and bruises covering my body, I couldn't wait to go back and do it all over again—I wanted another blackout. It allowed me to forget, to leave my body, to lose control.

From time to time, friends who never did drugs or drank the way I did have told me, "I don't like feeling out of control," explaining away the one time they got too drunk or took a drug. But that out-of-control feeling was what I strived for, I chased it. Today that's how I know I am an alcoholic and addict. "Normies" do not strive to lose all sense of themselves, all inhibition.

This type of risk-taking behavior did, of course, result in numerous situations you would never want to find yourself in. First, it was sneaking alcohol on the weekends when I was at parties with friends. We were in eighth grade so "parties" were hanging out in the forest with boys or walking around our little town until the 10:00 p.m. curfew. We smoked weed out of an apple (it can be done) and coordinated all of this through AOL Instant Messenger.

Us girls—we kissed *a lot* of boys. Kissing turned into making out, and as alcohol and drugs got introduced, I went further with my sexuality, becoming quite promiscuous but never going "all the way." I was fearful of real sex. I knew that whenever I went there for the first time, I would be expected to do it again. So

I chose instead to be a tease, pushing boundaries without ever moving past a certain line. This wasn't because I enjoyed teasing; I just thought it would make guys like me more. I wanted the validation of being sought after.

Looking back at photographs of that time, I can see I wasn't cute. I had braces and dressed like I had just walked out of a Hot Topic store (it was a thing at the time, I promise). I doubt these boys found me attractive, but they spotted something that could be preyed upon: vulnerability. They hooked up with me because they wanted a need met. That was the mentality I took into all sexual encounters. Drugs and alcohol allowed me to disassociate, to numb out, just to go through the motions. Because I thought that was what I was *supposed* to do.

When I was fourteen, I had my first "real" relationship. We were so young, but it was so serious. We spent every waking minute together. My parents were separating, and I wasn't home very often. Normally I wouldn't have been allowed to sleep at my boyfriend's house or be gone every single night of the week, but I think my parents had bigger things to worry about. Isaac came from a large family who welcomed me, and I went everywhere with them. His mom taught me to drive, and I spent many nights learning everything one doesn't need to know about *Halo* and *Call of Duty*. We dated for nearly two years before I found out he'd lost his virginity to one of my best friends.

I felt like I'd been punched in the stomach, and the feeling stayed for months. I told myself things like, "He probably wanted to stop dating me long before this but felt trapped, suffocated, and didn't want to hurt my feelings. I must be a bad girlfriend—or annoying. Why didn't I sleep with him first?" He never said these things to me, but I believed all of them as truth.

Then the comparison game started. I became obsessed with trying to find the differences and similarities between the girl he slept with and me. What did she have that I didn't? How could I make myself more like her? How could I make him stay? In this space I "learned" many ideas and foundational pieces that pushed me into the next stage of my life. Another part of me was also born in this season—the part that was afraid of being alone.

I'm glad I don't remember the conversation where I convinced him not to break up with me. It was probably pretty desperate. Nor do I recall exactly when I handed over *my* virginity. I was so hurt that I gave him the only thing I had left to give away, thinking it would seal the deal or something.

I must keep him, I thought, *so she can't have him.*

Unfortunately, I remember everything about the supposed "sacred" moment of having sex for the first time. Fourteen years old, in his grandparents' bed, our cheeks flushed, the cheesy country song humming in the background—and me slowly floating away. A skill I adapted with time and became good at. I figuratively left my body until I could "watch" what was happening as an onlooker. I hated every second of this experience and didn't realize until later that having sex with your boyfriend is not the answer to keeping him around.

***

In her book *How to Do the Work*, Dr. Nicole LePera describes dissociation as a maladaptive coping strategy, one that allows people to leave their bodies to avoid a stressful experience. She explains:

> Sexually this form of detachment can involve having sex with people we are not truly interested in. Instead,

it might involve dedicating ourselves to our partners'
pleasure without any awareness of or attention to our
own.[1]

I wanted to please *him*. To keep *him*. At the expense of
sacrificing myself. Unresolved trauma embeds itself in the very
being of who we are.

Losing my virginity didn't change anything except my self-
hatred. That grew. Alongside shame, regret, and that ache in my
stomach where I still felt like I'd been punched. Amanda, my ex-
friend who had slept with my boyfriend, made my life a living
hell. She would yell comments at me down the hall at school and
during football games. She used any chance she could to make me
feel uncomfortable. She didn't have to try hard; I was already *so*
uncomfortable in my skin. As the school's star running back, Isaac
scored touchdowns on the field, and Amanda would harass me in
the stands. She would write things on her Myspace page (wow,
I don't feel old or anything) that led me to believe she was still
talking to Isaac. It was a mind game. A psychological stronghold.

For the next three years, until the end of my junior year of high
school, he and I played the breakup game, cheated on each other,
and finally said goodbye. During those three years, I began to dabble
in cocaine and ecstasy, and I started smoking weed every day. My
inhibitions dropped. I grew numb to the constant ache inside me.

And I found somebody else. One of Isaac's friends and
teammates. Derek was the quarterback and sat in front of me in
geometry. (The only subject I ever got a B in. I blame him.) Isaac
was puppy love, but Derek was my first *real* love.

---

[1] Nicole LePera, *How to Do the Work: Recognize Your Patterns, Heal from Your Past, and Create* (New York: Harper Wave, 2021), 61.

As with many relationships, particularly the ones where drugs are involved, Derek and I had a lot of drama. Very high highs and very low lows. At times our relationship was emotionally taxing as we went through extreme attachment, instability, and codependency. The relationship would turn sour at the drop of a hat if one of us showed the *slightest* interest in somebody else. We were intensely jealous and unfortunately willing to cheat. He may have been acting out in an attempt to escape my destructive behaviors, the chaos I was addicted to, but somehow, someway, we always found the path back to each other.

As an athlete with college on the horizon, he was careful when it came to participating in my drug use. There were times when we were inseparable, but even those times proved to be toxic, as all I wanted to do was get high. Sitting in cars for hours doing lines, talking, watching the ocean, with Mac Dre playing in the background. How very California of us. When Derek didn't want to join me on my drug adventures, I would just find another guy to keep me company. I had an insatiable issue with being alone. Cocaine and Ecstasy became my very best friends.

Toward the end of my junior year of high school, my addiction really took off. I was doing eight balls of coke every day. It was during this phase that I once went along with Derek and some friends to pick up weed at an older guy's house; they exchanged and we left. After a few more trips to that house, I was able to get TK's number. He must have been in his mid-thirties, and I was sixteen or seventeen at the time. He began fronting me boats of ecstasy. For those who don't know, that means he would go to Oakland, buy a thousand ecstasy pills (thizzles for all my Bay Area people circa 2007), and essentially give them to me as long as I paid him back $2 per pill. I was selling these to everyone at our school for $10 to $15 a pop. Not everyone I went to school with was a drug addict, mind you, but we did get breathalyzed at every school dance or other event, so we took e-pills. I think my mom thought I was selling prom tickets because so many people came to our front door. Not my proudest moment.

This money fueled my drug addiction. Before the money started coming in, I stole, pawned different things, and used up every penny I ever made to buy coke. The drugs gave me a confidence I never actually possessed. I became a different person and lost all my true friends. People I had known my whole life. I began hanging out with the "outcasts" at school or the kids who had dropped out. All the girls hated me, and the guys liked me only because I was sleeping with them. I didn't even like sex, but I wanted the attention. I had a sick addiction to feeling desired.

By my senior year, I had one friend, and she didn't go to our school. Her name was Kristen. The rest of my associates were men. Or "boys," rather. Guys I knew I could manipulate with my body to get what I wanted. I had always been curvy, never skinny, but I began losing weight like crazy. I wouldn't eat all day, and the only food I did consume was microwave popcorn. My body must have been craving the salt. My mom thought I was on a "popcorn diet." In the evenings at the dinner table, I shoved pieces of her homemade meals into my napkin when she wasn't looking because I couldn't stomach them. I was flying way too high.

I distinctly remember how good I felt in my skin. False confidence ran through my veins. My clothes stopped fitting, and my weight loss became more and more apparent. One day I was walking down the main hall at school, and I heard a girl whisper, "It's like she loses weight over the weekend."

Of course, she knew *why* I was losing weight, and she clearly meant the comment to be an insult, but I loved it. This is where my food issues and body insecurities were born.

During one of our break-up-and-get-back-together times, Derek came over after school. We were both seniors and working on senior projects where we had to dress professionally and give a presentation. I was all "dressed up," and I showed him how my pants could quite possibly fit another person inside them. I thought my skinniness would be a turn-on, but he was not impressed. (Thanks, diet culture.) I was confused, as I had accepted the delusion that in the world, skinny meant sexy. As a young woman, on drugs or not, I thought "thin" was desirable.

I couldn't have been more wrong.

***

As a teenager, I took so many drugs that chasing a high began to lose its excitement. So I began chasing risk. I would put myself in dangerous situations, make poor choices, just to feel my heart pound in my chest—I liked that. My body began to crave the adrenaline just as much as any drug.

At seventeen, I would go to rap concerts in the Bay Area—sometimes with friends, sometimes not—and then turn around and leave with guys I met at the show. In 2016 I met some low-level rappers, and one began "grooming" me. His name was Andre. We would talk on the phone almost every night. As a teenager, I talked about teenage things, complaining about my home life, homework, and the drama with ex-friends. At the time, my parents were going through what I would call a midlife crisis. After they officially divorced, my dad quickly got remarried to a woman who was twenty years younger. My mom began dating and driving up to San

Francisco in the middle of the week, which left me alone in a quiet house with more than enough freedom to do exactly as I chose. I exposed myself and my vulnerabilities to an unsafe person who knew what to say to relate to my struggle, to pull at my heartstrings.

"Why don't you leave home for a couple of days and stay with me?" he'd say.

I began driving from Monterey, California, to Richmond and Vallejo, where I would dance on stage at Keak da Sneak concerts. I thought it was totally normal that I was with a guy who made me address him as "Daddy." The guys Andre and I hung out with had huge houses and nice cars, but I was far from safe. Everyone had guns, and every move I made was watched. I was out of my mind most of these trips to the Bay—so high that I didn't even know what drugs I was taking. I saw other girls at these houses and, at the time, figured they traveled with the rappers. One of the women did sing with their group, but something was off with all the other girls. They would look at me, and it seemed like their eyes were screaming, "Leave. Do not stay here." But their mouths wouldn't move. It was possible they were being pimped; if that was the case, they knew the potential consequences of telling me to go.

The addiction to danger came and went, ebbed and flowed. One morning during another visit to the Bay, the hour was early—before sunrise—and nobody else was awake. Who knows what led me to leave? To drive home in the pouring rain, never to speak to "Andre Daddy" again. But that's what happened.

As I type these words and read over them, I can't help but see this invisible protective orb that was around me. The situations I was in weren't pleasant, yet they could have been so much worse. Each time it's like I *just* managed to escape before the road took a darker turn.

CHAPTER 2

Pain demands to be felt—or it will demand you feel nothing at all.

—ANN VOSKAMP, *THE BROKEN WAY*

It wasn't easy getting drugs in our town. Especially hard drugs.

Eventually somebody introduced me to an older guy who came from a Sicilian family, and they were into some pretty dark stuff. The first few times I saw Josh, I was always with other people, but I began going to pick up coke by myself because I was selfish and didn't like to share. He took me to his family's home in Pasadena. I remember big staircases and marble floors. As we walked in the door, Josh came up behind me and pulled my shirt down to flash my boobs to his dad, who was leaning over the balcony.

Josh liked to bring me along with him to go get drugs. I, of course, wanted the drugs, not necessarily to hang out, but he never seemed to have coke when I arrived, which caused me to spend more time than I wanted with him. It was a game; he knew what I wanted and purposely took hours to get it, so I was forced to wait.

One night my friend Kristen was with us, and we pulled into an apartment complex where a car sat running in the carport. Josh just hopped in the driver's seat and stole the car. He yelled for one of us to follow him, and I jumped in the passenger's seat of a stolen vehicle without even thinking about it. We drove around aimlessly, without any purpose for this crime, until he finally ditched the car; I then returned to my car and took Kristen home.

The very next day, I went to pick up again.

I don't know why I never purchased drugs in larger quantities. Maybe it was to limit myself, so I wouldn't do it all. An interesting thought, since I had a restricted mindset around food as well, long into my adult years. Probably some false attempt at trying to control what little I could control in my chaotic life.

Josh told me to meet him at his grandmother's house, where I had never been. As soon as I walked inside, he locked the door. Then he threw me on the bed and raped me.

This is what happens to girls like me, I thought. *I was flirting with him.* I'd been trying to score some free coke or have him give me a deal—anything, but I guessed I took it too far, led him on, so he finally took what he wanted.

Am I a tease? I guess this is my fault. Thoughts raced through my head. I didn't tell anyone what happened, and I didn't think anything of the fact that I was a minor. I simply assumed that what happened to me was a symptom of the life I was choosing to live. A symptom of the drug world. He had something I wanted, and I obviously had something he wanted, but instead of asking me for it, he just took it. And I was too scared to say anything.

After he raped me, it was like nothing happened. I continued to ride around in the car with him, doing lines of coke and staying with him. My legs were shaking, something that used to happen a lot when I was younger and about to do something I shouldn't, like make out with a boy or smoke weed in the woods with my friends. Eventually, as I continued to participate in risky behavior, I managed to silence this "warning" signal from my body. But this particular night my body was screaming, and I ended up having a cocaine-induced seizure. Looking back now, I think it must have been a combination of the drugs and the sexual assault. My nervous system in overdrive finally tapped out.

I had been exhibiting over-sexualized behavior for a while, which is a trauma impact symptom. Exploiters know how to take advantage of this type of trauma response, and they can influence how youth understand what is happening to them and why. This is referred to as sexual reactivity/trauma and can oftentimes lead youth to engage other youth in sexual activity later on.

***

Later that day, Josh took me to a meth house.

I will never forget what the inside of that large Victorian home looked like. On the first floor, two women shared a tiny bedroom, and a gay man with dreads lived in the bigger bedroom. He had kind eyes. He recognized how young I was, and when I asked for a hit from his pipe, he told me, "You do not want this life."

I thought what I needed was more drugs, but they knew I needed food and gave me a bowl of pasta and some milk.

This was the first time I had seen anyone do meth. Josh snorted a line and then went off somewhere, leaving me at the house. Completely spun out, I tried to explain to the others what had happened earlier that day. I thought Josh was going to hurt me again. Overwhelmed, I started crying and hid in the bathroom.

When one of the women asked if I wanted a line, I took it willingly, and it instantly masked the pain.

"We need to go get more," they said.

I handed over some money and the two women left. If you know anything about meth, tweakers don't do anything fast. These women were gone all day.

The woman who rented the upstairs didn't do drugs and had a young boy probably around five years old. It didn't matter how far gone I was; even on drugs, I had this spot in my heart for children. One of the other ladies also had a child. The little girl was so cute, with missing teeth and deep red hair. She soaked up the attention I gave her.

I spent the night at the house, and the next morning, I realized the food they had given me was the last of what they had. I tried to find some breakfast for the little girl, and there was *nothing* in the cupboards. She didn't even have a toothbrush. Her mom wasn't going to take her to school, so I drove her to *my* mom's house. I sneaked in through the window to grab a toothbrush and took the girl to school.

Then I returned to the Victorian house and waited.

Time passes on methamphetamine—without sleep, without eating, without the normal things your body requires of you. Your body's needs are silenced by the powerful adrenaline coursing through your veins. I'm not sure how many days passed, but eventually I went home again. I'm sure my mom thought I'd been hanging out with friends. That was the story I sold her, anyway. After picking every single blackhead, existent and nonexistent, out of my nose until my skin was raw, I lay awake all night.

To prove how young I was at this time, I was trying to sleep in a bedroom that had hot pink walls, and I was wearing my retainer. For the next eight hours, I sucked my teeth so hard that the retainer closed the tiny gap between my front teeth by the time the sun came up. I could not rest. Josh relentlessly texted me all night long, and I kept thinking I heard his ringtone outside my window and became convinced he was on the roof. This easily could have been the drugs talking, but that was the kind of man Josh was; he might have done something like that. I was so scared that I went into my brother's room and peered out the window, where I spotted a black Suburban out on the street—one of the cars that had been at the Victorian house. My brother was only ten or eleven at the time, but terrified, I woke him up and lay down at the foot of his bed.

When I heard my mom leave for the gym at 5:30 that morning, I called the police, convinced Josh was at my house.

They came and took a report. I showed them the text messages on my phone where he was threatening me, and because of his record and possibly an open investigation, they were highly interested in this information. But when they did a perimeter check, they didn't find anything. He wasn't there.

I was wearing a baby pink sweatshirt, standing there shaking from the meth and fear, and I looked like a young vulnerable girl. I wanted to tell the police that he raped me, but it was like the words were trapped in my throat. I felt I deserved what happened because of this drug life I had chosen to live.

The sky was still dark when my mom returned, and she completely freaked out when she saw the police cars at our house. We stayed that night in a hotel.

"What happened to your nose?" she asked.

17

I don't remember what lame excuse I used, but I do remember spending the entire fifteen-minute drive to the hotel ducked down in the backseat of her car, fear pumping through me. I refused to sit in the front seat. My hands shook, and I desperately wanted a cigarette. I thought I saw Josh in every single car we passed.

***

During my last semester in high school, I began writing myself "passes" to leave school. I was an office teacher's assistant, and I used to steal anything and everything. So I would write myself a pass and go home and do line after line of coke instead of attending class.

When graduation day arrived, I didn't even want to go. I had lost so much weight that my pastel green dress hung limply on my shoulders. Looking in the mirror, I whispered, "What's the point?"

I had grown up with a small class of roughly a hundred people since I was five, yet I had zero friends at the end of this milestone. Zero people I wanted to hug and say congratulations to. Deep down I loved several of the girls I'd grown up with. Many of my guy friends used to be at my house every night playing basketball in the yard. The drugs, however, told me I hated these people and they hated me. I was combative and told my mom I wasn't going to walk across that stage.

Despite my lifestyle, I somehow managed to graduate with a 4.0 GPA, but I had missed so much school that the vice principal warned me with a visit to my house. "You will not be able to walk at the graduation ceremony if you miss another class," he said.

I regretted not ditching the last day of school.

CHAPTER 2

The majority of my fellow classmates had done a number to their brains with the ecstasy tablets I'd sold them that year. Following our graduation, they danced around to "Sandstorm" and threw their caps while I blacked out. The next thing I remember, I was home at my graduation party, attempting to drink champagne out of the bottle and opening gift after gift like a spoiled brat. I received Tiffany bracelets and charms, a camera, and a trip to Japan.

And all I wanted to do was leave with my one friend, who didn't graduate, and go fill my nose with white powder. I was in and out of consciousness, but I remember that things got really ugly. Cussing, screaming, physical aggression—all toward my family who just wanted to help me.

I ran away for two weeks.

The night my mom convinced me to come home, I was rolling on more than enough e-pills. I had been doing lines of cocaine all day, and when I arrived at the house, my dad was there, my brother was awake, and I was too messed up to put the pieces together. I didn't find it weird that my divorced parents and eleven-year-old brother were all awake and waiting for me at the insane hour when I finally got home.

The next thing I knew, strangers were hauling me from my bed. A husky blonde woman and a huge guy transported me to the airport, and I was on my way to rehab. So much for Japan. They took me to Cottonwood, a residential treatment center in Tucson, Arizona, where I was placed on the adolescent side of the facility because I was two months shy of turning eighteen. It was 110 degrees and raining, with cacti and tarantulas everywhere.

I did not want to be in the desert. I did not want to be housed with thirteen-year-old girls in rooms made of plastic windows.

19

I did not want to recite the alphabet every time I went to the bathroom to assure everybody I was, in fact, *not* throwing up my food. I wanted a freaking cigarette.

I quickly learned that having a bad attitude would not allow me to leave this place any sooner, so I did the work. I participated and listened and got a taste for all things program related. However, after accumulating forty-five days sober, I had a severe stress response and ended up getting shingles. If you know anything about shingles, it's basically the chickenpox virus and usually affects the elderly. It lies dormant in our systems to emerge with a vengeance, sending pulsating shocks through different parts of the body's nerves. Normal people are prescribed pain killers, codeine, etc. Well, I was seventeen and in a drug rehab center, so I was gifted with ibuprofen and a two-week quarantine.

While I missed obstacle courses, equine therapy, and recovery meetings, I read a book called *The Power of Now* by Ekhart Tolle. I began to learn what it means to stay in the present moment. I felt myself coming back into my body for the first time since age ten, and I began this practice of acknowledging and accepting the simplicity of the moment. Of the here and now. I believe that's what got me through the rest of my stay at Cottonwood.

***

My parents prayed and hoped that Cottonwood would be a "quick fix" for me. A short time after I returned home, I left again, this time for Long Beach State University. I looked presentable, so I was good—right? Everyone collectively held their breath. I was like a package, shipped off to Southern California with a giant bow on top. Yet the bow served only to cover up the bright red rehab tape barely holding the box together.

Recovery is never linear, and as much as we wish rehab were a magic button we could press and make everything okay again— that's not how it works. I was seven hours away from home in a new city, on a giant college campus. Navigating Long Beach State was like swimming in a sea of 35,000 students, and I was the only one who didn't receive the instruction manual. My classes were practically out on the beach. I did not have a car, a longboard, or a bike like some of the other students did, and my schedule had weird blocks between classes where I didn't have time to walk the distance back to my dorm, only to turn around and walk back to the beach an hour later for my next class. I didn't know where the library or student center was. I didn't have a meal plan or know where to do my laundry; I actually didn't even know these things were available to me. I felt lost, detached, unworthy, not smart enough, not pretty enough, and not capable enough to go to college. I knew the voice speaking to me, and I knew how to silence it. So I did the only thing I *did* know how to do, and that was drink and use.

To this day, I have no idea how people can party *and* attend college without failing their classes. The way I like to drink? It just isn't possible. I was blackout drinking, waking up to my bed sheets soaked in urine. I stopped attending class and started pulling out the only money I had to support myself with so I could buy cocaine.

One morning I woke up in a random girl's dorm room, with people spread out all over the floor like zombies. I didn't remember how I got there, my lip was swollen and bloody, and my body ached. As I tried to walk back to my own room, I came to the conclusion that I had been sexually assaulted. The awareness shook me.

Two girls I went to high school with lived on the floor below me. Still intoxicated, I managed to convince them to let me borrow their car. I'm not sure if I told them my plan or if they just thought I was going to the gas station down the street, but I took off for Sacramento. I wanted safety—to be somewhere I felt fully known. I wanted Derek.

I recall making it to the first stoplight on Lakewood Boulevard and pulling onto the freeway. I had to close one eye because I was seeing double, and I accidentally got off the freeway at the very next exit. Confused out of my mind, I drove in a literal circle, getting on and off the freeway. What a blessing it was that I couldn't figure out how to navigate right then because I could have really hurt somebody or myself. I was so frustrated, defeated, and I did not want this feeling of intoxication any longer—I wanted clarity. Everything felt foggy.

The next morning, I took an Amtrak train all the way from Long Beach to Sacramento. The longest train ride ever. After a weekend there, it wasn't long before I dropped out of school and moved back home to the Monterey Peninsula. For a while, I tried to go to the local junior college. I enrolled in some random health class, but even then I felt like something was missing. There must be something wrong with *me*, because I just didn't get this whole "school" thing. A guy in my class invited me to a party at his house that night. I went to the party and never went back to class.

Constantly I felt like I had a giant target on my forehead and all men knew they could approach me, get something from me, and dispose of me when they were done. Each time I thought it wouldn't happen again, it did. My vulnerabilities were on display for any manipulative abuser to spot. They somehow knew, "This one is easy prey."

CHAPTER 2

Traffickers normally go after "new" victims versus chasing the ones who leave. Of course, this is not always the case, but it helps explain why I continually felt pursued by a variety of unsafe men. It's easier to woo a new girl and convince her to stay than to chase after one who has uncovered the truth about who you really are and try to convince her otherwise.

CHAPTER 3

The human spirit is virtually indestructible,
and its ability to rise from the ashes remains
as long as the body draws breath.

—ALICE MILLER

Oxycontin is an expensive habit.

In general, drugs can rack up expenses, and I had my fair share of each one, but this little pill I was attracted to—well, I could not maintain the habit for long. Five months had passed since I graduated high school, and in that time, I'd been sent to rehab in Arizona, dropped out of two colleges, and begun using again. I felt displaced and disconnected from any type of progressional trajectory for my life. I was just simply existing, without purpose.

This time I asked to go to treatment.

Recovery is a funny thing. You can want the best for somebody and watch as they burn their life to the ground, but until *they* want help—until they choose—there is usually nothing you can do. I moved down to Southern California for the second time that year. This time to enter a women's treatment program called Safe Harbor.

The setup was two adjoining houses with a huge backyard. Fifteen girls shared the space. I was reluctant to get sober, kicking myself the whole drive down with my mom, hearing my addict brain scream, "Why did you ask for help? Now look at you going to rehab—again!" I told myself, "I should have gotten high one last time."

But eventually I adjusted and stayed in inpatient treatment for three months. I learned to hide my cigarettes underneath my bunk bed, and each morning when I got on my knees to retrieve them, I felt a subtle reminder to pray. I was confronted with my younger self in a series of therapeutic exercises that I would encounter again and again throughout my journey of healing. Finally I formed fifteen friendships with women my age, who were all doing the same thing—trying to rebuild their lives.

After the initial ninety days, I moved into a sober living house that offered more freedom but still provided the parameters and safety of a program environment. Eventually I got an apartment in Newport Beach with two other girls from the program.

In Orange County at the time, the culture for young people was you were in a twelve-step program or you were drunk. I was surrounded by eighteen- to thirty-year-olds who were all doing the deal, and we managed to live happy, joyous, and free. I went to meetings, went to school, got my esthetics license at Paul Mitchell, had a sponsor, and worked the steps.

But I did not believe in "God." Instead, I chose Mother Nature. For a while, I didn't wear any shoes so I could become one with the earth. I believed in the law of attraction and the power of the universe; I practiced Reiki, charged crystals, and even questioned a Ouija board. That was the season I was in, and it worked for me until it didn't.

I did everything I could to try and find *something* that would satisfy that place inside of me, the place the program talks about: a gaping hole that longs to be filled. I wouldn't learn this until much later, but ultimately that place for me could be filled only with Jesus.

***

I met a guy. He was twenty-six, charming, artistic—and sober. I clearly remember going to meetings and locking eyes with him. His silent pursuit excited me, and at nineteen years old, I got caught up in attraction and the thrill of possibly being desired. I certainly didn't realize the danger I was about to step into.

His name was Rory, and he managed to fool everybody, including my friends and family. We moved in together right away, and he immediately sold his vehicle so we had to share mine. He started asking to see my phone. In the beginning, these were just little things, but he began flirting with other girls in front of me, communicating with them online, spinning me into a rage of jealousy. That's when the gaslighting began. When I tried to confront him, he told me I was "crazy" and "overreacting."

Internal warning bells started going off when I discovered his dark and severe addiction to pornography. I wanted him to love *me*, not the girls on the screen. My desperation for his attention and approval grew, and he knew it. He would tell me, "You could look like the girls on the screen if you wanted to," which later led to his suggesting I do porn. "You could make us a lot of money." That's when the countless photoshoots began to take place; he made videos of us having sex and took me to plastic surgeons' offices. I would get callbacks from porn agents, and my legs shook as I answered the phone and began talking to these predators. My nervous system screamed at me, "*Do not go to that meeting.*"

Like all addictions, Rory's addiction to sex began to increase. Today it is wild to think of him as my boyfriend, especially now that I know what he really was. "My boyfriend" is another false narrative I chose to accept as reality. We had a bond and bonds equal survival. I would have done anything to keep that unhealthy bond with him, even if it meant betraying myself. I acted in a way that was counterintuitive to who I truly was, just so he would love me.

He began bringing people home from bars to sleep with and, of course, make videos of it. I knew if I refused to participate, there would be consequences, one being that I would have to sit there and watch the person I loved have sex with somebody else. I couldn't bear it.

Sexual encounters with strangers were like an addiction in itself for him. He had profiles on multiple dating websites at the same time he was going to bars and nightclubs to pick up new encounters. Meanwhile, I waited in our apartment as his personal chauffeur and designated driver, since I was too young to go with him. He would call and tell me to come pick them up—him and his companion from the bar—and I couldn't choose to be unavailable. I didn't have friends he "approved" of, and I wasn't allowed to have hobbies, because if I did, I might not be there when he called. I always had to be ready.

He began advertising me on Craigslist. People would pay to watch him and I have sex, or he would watch them have sex with me. People were purchasing these acts that all involved me, but I never saw a dime. This was about the time I began using again.

***

Each time I began using drugs, my addiction came back harder and stronger. The Bible describes this with a tiny story often called "The Return of the Unclean Spirit." The Amplified version puts it this way:

> Then it goes and brings with it seven other spirits more wicked than itself, and they go in and make their home there. And the last condition of that man becomes worse than the first. So will it also be with this wicked generation. (Matthew 12:45 AMP)

I began using the only drug I had never tried: heroin. Those spirits came and I was trapped.

Life with Rory was a constant betrayal of myself. I slowly began abandoning who I was and what I knew to be real in order to be who he wanted me to be. It was like I was extinguishing myself—I was a fire that needed to be put out. I had to conform to his model so I could shine brightly for the performance. But not in real life. I had to completely dim my light to meet the comfort of others.

What I was witnessing, feeling, and having to do—heroin numbed these things for me. It allowed me to abandon and betray myself without experiencing all the guilt. The person who once "wooed" me with his charm no longer expressed interest in me. Some days he ignored me completely, which was painful in itself. A loss of relationship. But the expectation remained that I would perform intimate acts to please him. The whole situation was confusing, especially to my heart, which knew a different version of love had to exist.

I had to do a lot of nasty things with a lot of nasty people in order to get the drugs I craved. I began asking homeless strangers to shoot me up and would go places I knew I shouldn't just to pick up my next fix. I was allowing people to see my body and "find a vein," but they were just creeps who wanted me to take my pants off. My skin itched so badly that I began to bruise all over, and trying to hide the bruises from Rory was almost impossible. I reached a point where I truly believed the heroin was "helping" me.

Rory quit his normal job to do tattoos out of our home. This created more opportunities for unknown strangers to come in, take their clothes off, and for me to say nothing. I was tired of saying nothing. When he decided to quit his job, I was working two jobs, one of which was with his family. He would drive me to work in my car, pick me back up, and take my phone when we got home. He controlled every aspect of my life. At nineteen, I was codependently supporting a twenty-six-year-old sex addict—and, though I didn't have the language for this yet, a trafficker.

Especially when he was absent or showed me a lack of affection, I believed the lies he engrained inside me. I "built" myself up with the words I heard him say time and time again. "You were meant to work in the sex industry. This is how you make money—by making men happy." I thought that was my purpose—to make *others* happy through the use of my body.

Rory was a master manipulator. He was selling me on the internet and, at the same time, promising to marry me and have children with me. He truly did want a family. He'd throw my birth control away for months at a time, and I remember thinking that maybe if I had a baby with him, he might love me again. I seriously wondered if this weird sexual part of our life would end once I became a mom. Maybe then he would see me in that role: a loving caretaker. A life-giver. Instead of an object.

Dr. Nicole LePera says, "The hormones released during sex have a similar effect as a pain killer."[1] As I engaged in these sexual practices with Rory, it masked the unwanted feelings I had toward him and the abuse he inflicted. For the moment, sex acted like a sedative. Hurt didn't exist as long as I was giving my body over to him. I didn't understand how much I was settling for a cheap version, a superficial cover-up, to real love and intimacy. I settled into the darkness and let the "painkiller" do its job, washing over me.

Emotions show up after sex. Confusion began to arise within me as I struggled to maintain any form of sobriety. I half-heartedly attempted to convince myself that Rory and I would one day have a happily ever after. But what I saw with us didn't fit the ever-after stories I knew. It actually didn't look like *anyone's* life I knew. Men purchased me daily, and my "boyfriend" was okay with me meeting men—*old* men—in hotel rooms, their cars, and their homes.

***

God had not yet revealed Himself to me, but today I recognize that He was the One who nudged me. I had muffled my spirit since I was a little girl, but one day it rose up within me and gave me unusual strength.

When I woke up that morning, the day seemed as ordinary as any other. But for some reason, the delusion I was living in became crystal clear. I saw things the way they actually were, and the decision I made was solid. Nothing muddied. Assurance filled my chest.

I called home.

---

[1] LePera, *How to Do the Work*, 138.

I didn't tell my mother everything. Quite frankly, this book may be the first time my mom learns the truth about what happened. But she drove six hours to reach me. I quit both of my jobs, sold my car, packed up half of the apartment. I was shaking, pleading to a God I didn't *quite* believe in, hoping Rory didn't walk through the door.

I was able to transfer the apartment into his name. At his suggestion, I had taken out everything in my name: the apartment lease, credit cards, the car. I hadn't thought anything of it at the time, but knowing what I know now about the judicial system and about traffickers, this was another cunning way for him to go undetected and keep his hold on me.

My mom arrived, not knowing the full extent of the relationship. She just helped me move home again to the Monterey Peninsula.

CHAPTER 4

Let go or be dragged.

—ZEN PROVERB

After leaving Orange County, I had no idea what to do.

Rory didn't allow me to walk away easily. He pleaded with me to come back, pretending to be everything I ever wanted him to be. He knew the right words and told me all the things I wanted to hear. Intense pain pierced my heart, and I felt like I was going to shatter into a million fragmented pieces. As I sobbed day after day, I kept thinking about going back to him. Maybe this time things would be different. Maybe he realized life without me wasn't what he wanted and everything would change for the better.

That, of course, was a lie: a false narrative that victims of abuse tend to believe. We convince ourselves it is the truth. Statistics say that sex trafficking victims will return to their former life six or seven times before leaving for good. One reason this happens is false narratives. This was the first time I was faced with making decisions on my own. Rory had made so many decisions for me, and I lacked the self-assurance to make them myself.

"What do you want for dinner?" Mom would ask.

Just a simple question. But I would feel my body start to shake, and I'd burst into tears. I was damaged and weak, which is where many victims find themselves and consequently make the decision to return to what they had before. We convince ourselves it wasn't so bad, that at least our basic needs were met. And the worst part: "He loves me. It would be better to go back to him."

Weak, damaged, and vulnerable people are sold the idea that they could never make it on their own. They don't have the strength to provide for or protect themselves. Even after everything I'd gone through with him, I genuinely thought I *needed* Rory. I was searching for something, grasping for anything, and I was trauma-bonded to my abuser.

If not for my family's support, I think I would have gone back. Much like the Israelites when they left Egypt, survivors of abuse can forget how bad it was under the yoke of slavery; their brains romanticize the past and keep showing them the times they were provided and cared for. The brain cannot show the unknown as truth, because the unknown is a maybe. A fantasy. Going back to what *I knew* seemed more appealing than walking around in the desert of the unknown.

When Rory realized his attempts to win me back weren't working, he tried a different approach. "I'm on my way. I am driving there, and I'm going to hurt you and your family."

I wasn't sure I believed him. I didn't trust his words—he wasn't a violent man—but it was still unsettling. Especially when he gave me time updates: "I'm two hours away staying in a hotel for the night, but in the morning…"

CHAPTER 4

I wanted to call his bluff, but my family was not convinced he was lying. So I filed for a restraining order.

***

Nobody wakes up one day and decides, "I'm going to be a prostitute." There is always something, perhaps a series of events, that leads someone down the path of prostitution. I don't believe it's a personal choice. When you run out of options, there are no choices.

According to Treasures, a nonprofit that empowers survivors of the trafficking and commercial sex industries, 89 percent of women want to leave prostitution, but they see no other option for survival.[1] Some need to provide for themselves and their children. For me and many others, we were exploited first, and the exploitation opened the door to the idea of selling my body. Not many people understand that 84 percent of women in prostitution are being trafficked by a third party; they're trapped in "the life" due to vulnerability and a lack of alternatives, and they are conditioned to protect that third party at all costs.

If not for the prior exploitation, I never would have stepped into life as an escort. It wouldn't have been on the table at all. But Rory had devalued me again and again, and my self-esteem was scraping the bottom of the river. I believed that I was doing exactly what I was meant to do. I hated it, but I was convinced that my purpose was to give men whatever *they* desired. I told myself the same lies Rory had fed me for years. I was *meant* to work in the sex industry—and he had taught me how.

On a search for heroin, I rediscovered meth, and from that point on, I was swallowed up by the fragmented dissolution that

---

[1] Harmony (Dust) Grillo, "Should Prostitution Be Decriminalized?," Treasures, accessed Nov. 26, 2021, https://www.iamatreasure.com/blog/should-prostitution-be-legal.

is the meth world. The not-eating, not-sleeping, rapid-weight-loss, adrenaline-pumping meth world. I read somewhere that methamphetamine is like being on a spiritual fast for Satan. The second I used it, all the chaos surrounding me ceased. Everything was okay. I felt better, and I could talk about everything that had happened with Rory and it finally made sense in my head. In the beginning, before the drug sunk its teeth into me, I felt like I could get so much accomplished. But I got down to ninety pounds. I was picking my skin all over; when I looked at myself in the mirror, I could see blood splatters on the glass. I looked ill. I looked old. A ghost of a girl stared back at me.

In this place of chaos and drug-induced peace, I began browsing the sexual services/encounters section on Craigslist because I thought that was the only way I could make money. Though I no longer had a trafficker telling me what to do, my trauma had not been addressed and it led me to do what I knew. I kept building myself into the person Rory had wanted me to be, changing my exterior to fit the mold of what he said was "desirable." Numbing my interior in order to participate in the world I "belonged" in. Allowing his words to permeate my brain, long after he was gone.

I ended up getting involved with an escort service. The fact that this even existed in a place like Monterey County was news to me. We didn't have strip clubs or even real nightclubs. There were no bars with young shot girls or poles. Eventually I realized these "businesses" do exist here, but they are just hidden.

A woman ran the escort service. I spoke to her on the phone maybe one time, and after that encounter she remained behind the scenes. Also hidden, like her business. Since the person in charge was essentially unavailable, the business operated this way: The girls with the most seniority trained the new girls. Simple as that. "It's mainly just dancing for parties," they told me.

I could do that, I thought, working to believe the bald-faced lie. I smiled and answered, "No problem." Dancing was so much better than any of the other things Rory had made me do.

Dancing at parties didn't exactly cover the whole job description, but the money *was* great. We had clients in Carmel and Pebble Beach—this wasn't some low-budget operation. But let me be clear: Even high-end escorts have a boss. And when those who work in the sex industry have a boss, it is probable that force, fraud, and coercion will occur, which defines human trafficking according to federal law.

Over time as trust was built, I was given clients out of town. I began driving to Sacramento and San Jose and was assigned to men in those regions. I preferred this; being a Monterey County native, I didn't want to run into anybody local. On these trips up north, I was not allowed to give my information to the men, nor were they able to give me theirs. They were loyal to my boss. One time I asked "Tim" from Sacramento, "Why don't you give me your number and we can meet privately?"

He quickly got nervous. "I'm not allowed to do that."

I'm not sure what type of fear tactics this organization used on the buyers, but the buyers did not stray from the contract.

I lost all touch with myself, bypassing my body's warning signals, and simply accepted my role as a "sex worker." Every night I was required to drop off a percentage of the money I earned. I would walk down a dark alley in historic downtown Monterey to hand over a portion of what I'd made that night. Dirty money passed through a window from me to the girl managing the phone lines. She barely batted an eyelash as I handed her the envelope. Things began to shift, and they began keeping more and more of my earnings.

I was twenty years old and hated myself.

***

Trauma physically changes the brain. Research shows that trauma causes the brain to alter its stress response system, which in turn causes a shift in the way information is filtered.

That explains a lot about why I responded, or *didn't* respond, in multiple instances where I felt threatened. Having lived in a hypervigilant state for most of my adolescent and early adult life, I kept repeating the same behaviors and finding myself in the same dangerous places. The men I attracted were all the same, just in different bodies. It was like I couldn't learn from past mistakes and had no ability to discern anything. Time after time I found myself in exploitative scenarios, and now I know this happened because of my vulnerabilities and the way trauma was stored in my brain.

I did not enjoy these events, nor did I seek them out. I wasn't a bad person, nor did I lack willpower. But my brain was altered. People kept my pay; men forced me to do things I didn't want to do, but that was just the nature of "the game."

I had one real friend. Her name was Nicole, and we were inseparable. All I wanted was to find some heroin and check out, but meth was more accessible. So she and I exchanged checking out for being "up up up."

***

The meth world was the same as I remembered back in high school, from that one night with Josh. The same dark hum permeated the places and people who used it. The familiar undertone made my legs shake. Paranoia mixed with adrenaline caused me to feel like I was always on a mission, constantly on alert.

My friend Nicole was the only person who knew I was working for an escort service. She was the only one I allowed into that part of my life. I supported her financially and definitely supported her drug habit. We did everything together, including a lot of meth.

One day we met a guy at a gas station. Isn't it strange how people doing dirt find each other? Dru introduced us to his plug: an older white lady named Michelle. She seemed extremely happy to meet us, likely because we would be buying drugs from her.

I quickly learned that Michelle was a self-proclaimed escort but didn't really work anymore.

"Now I have other girls," she said, casually taking ownership.

No red flags. No gut intuition pinging madly inside me when I heard this. I just smiled and kept abandoning myself. *Ash, you're doing great.*

Over time we got to know Michelle better. One particular night, Nicole, a sort-of friend named Dani, and I all piled in my car, with Michelle sitting in the front seat giving directions. She was taking us to meet her "friend." Years later I realized the house we pulled up to was on the *same block* as my mom's house, but I was too spun out even to notice. Michelle brought all three of us girls to the front door and knocked.

I'd gone from brunette to blonde when Rory convinced me I needed to look more like a porn star. Now I was platinum blonde with green and blue pieces, and I might have been a hundred pounds dripping wet. Skin and bones, but you couldn't tell me I didn't look good. I thought I looked incredible, when in reality, I was a shell of a person.

A man answered the door.

"Take your pick," Michelle said, pointing at the three of us girls huddled on his doorstep.

I think we all stood a little straighter in that moment, wanting to please "Mom." When the man didn't pick me, I felt crushed. My self-esteem told me I'd been rejected, and I immediately went into comparison mode, piling up all the reasons this stranger didn't think I was pretty enough, attractive enough, sexy enough. In some sick, twisted way, I wanted to be chosen.

"The life" has a way of manipulating your thinking. Looking back now, I can see that the fact this man didn't pick me meant I didn't get sold that night. It meant I didn't have to engage sexually with somebody I didn't even know. It meant I didn't get raped and objectified, for somebody else's profit. Not getting chosen *saved* me, but I didn't see it that way.

***

Nicole and I invested in a lot of darkness around this time. Not only were we involved in the escort service, but we also had a friend who was washing money. Loaded up with a bunch of fake bills—twenties converted into hundreds—we took a trip to Santa Cruz in my white Mercedes SUV. Bingo scratch-off tickets littered my backseats, and dope lines perfectly placed on a CD rested on top of my center console. We were two very lost girls who had an affinity for Bay Area rap music and reckless behavior. We pulled up to a dingy little motel across from The Catalyst Club and parked.

At the club, we sang along as a group of Bay Area rappers performed. Popping a few ecstasy pills, we danced around as our responsibilities and inhibitions vanished in a cloud of club smoke.

We had this unspoken understanding between us; our mission was to catch the attention of the guys on stage. We weren't twenty-one and couldn't drink, but we had plans to party that night.

As we walked back to the hotel, hoping to get a little bump up our noses before heading back out for the night, a black Escalade pulled up. I ignored the catcalls from inside until Nicole exclaimed, "That's JT!"[2]

JT was one of the original Oakland rappers associated with Mac Dre. I don't know how Nicole recognized him inside the car or why all of a sudden it was now okay to climb in with him and his friends, but that's what we did. We pulled into a parking lot with all the other performers and entertainers.

As JT rolled a Backwood, I jokingly said in a sing-song voice, "I smoke Backwood blunts cuz they the most expensive." A Mac Dre lyric.

They exclaimed, "Ohh, these white girls are with the shit."

Good, I thought. *I impressed them.*

And then they took us to their hotel room.

***

Strangely enough, there were times when it seems like my addiction to meth caused me to avoid dangerous situations. I was so spun out that night that I never followed through with the offers presented to me.

"I have a house in Vegas," JT explained. "You could make so much money out there. Have you ever danced before?"

I had already made up my mind to leave Monterey. I didn't have a plan yet, or a destination, but I knew I wanted out of the

---

[2] This is a pseudonym. It is possible you would recognize this rapper's real name.

escort service because it was tearing me apart. I wanted to move somewhere that had strip clubs. (I don't know why I thought a strip club would be the answer, but I digress.) I perked up when he mentioned the word *dance*.

He continued, "You should at least come check it out. I have eight other girls that live with me, a huge house, lots of rooms. Pick one and it's yours. Las Vegas is poppin'!"

I told him I had never been.

"No? Ah man, you gotta come with me. What else do you have to do? I'll buy your ticket. You just let me know when."

He sold it to me like it was a mansion in Beverly Hills. I thought about all the money I could make and how it would be all mine. *Just dancing*, I thought. *No sex*. Naive as to who was really going to be keeping the profit. Naive also to how strip clubs operate. Compared to what I had to do at the escort service, I thought this offer sounded pretty good. I told him I would think about it.

Most drugs are captivating, but meth consumes you. And that is where I landed for most of my addiction. I never went to Las Vegas—thankfully, because looking back now, I see that JT was grooming me. And he did not let up for a while. He'd call me regularly and tell me the offer still stood, and he'd talk about buying me plane tickets and kept promising this glamorous lifestyle. I equaled dollar signs to him, not the other way around.

***

Somewhere during this time, I got a new idea. A brilliant, meth-induced epiphany that I should go to Europe with nothing but a backpack of clothes and stay in hostels and explore the world.

Sitting at our kitchen counter one night, I said, "Mom, it's like this. If I put good energy out there, I will meet exactly the right people and be taken care of! It's like that one time in high school when I wanted to join the Peace Corps and build huts in Africa."

My mom almost fell out of her seat. Struggling to gain composure, she said, "Absolutely not, Ash. This is not like the Peace Corps. *That* time all I had to tell you was that there were giant bugs in Africa!"

She looked close to losing it, so I stopped pressing. I was a lost daughter, a lost soul, and reaching for anything that would transport me to somewhere new, where I could maybe *be* someone new.

When my phone rang one day and my high-school boyfriend Derek suggested I move to Missouri with him, I jumped at the chance.

***

Derek had gone out there to play football. We weren't together anymore, but we were friends, and over the years our lives overlapped several times. When he saw me again, I didn't look like the girl he used to know, and I think he was concerned. He probably thought this move would help me get off the drugs, experience the wholesomeness of the Midwest, and settle down. Maybe I would find some purpose for my currently worthless existence.

I didn't bother to visit first. I just made plans to move. To leave the escort service behind forever.

The last time I saw Tim, my Sacramento client, I told him I was moving to Missouri because my mom was sick, not because a boy had invited me. What kind of person makes up a lie like that?

Tim had been requesting to see me more and more frequently, and whenever I said I couldn't drive to Sac, he began traveling to me. He would get rooms at some of the nicest places on the Peninsula: rooms that were $1,300 a night kind of nice. But also directly in my hometown. I felt sick walking into the lobby, all eyes peeled in my direction. Sometimes I had trouble finding his room, which just made everything worse. I felt so disgusted with myself and the way I was dressed. *What am I doing here?* I wondered.

The last time he requested me, he asked me to stay the night, but I refused. As I walked the cobblestone pathway from his room to my car, I could hear the ocean crashing in the distance. I stared down at the dirty money in my hands and collapsed to the ground crying.

CHAPTER 5

Painful as it may be, a significant emotional event can be the catalyst for choosing a direction that serves us and those around us more effectively. Look for the learning.

—LOUISA MAY ALCOTT

Without even thinking about it, I moved across the country.

I had blonde-and-blue hair, piercings, and was covered in tattoos, and Missouri was shocked to see me. I felt the same way about Missouri—one of my first days there, it was twenty-two degrees and the wind felt like tiny paper cuts to the face. I had no connections, no purpose. Just a suitcase and a $400 apartment.

Right after I moved, the 2011 Tohoku earthquake struck Japan, and I remember questioning God as I watched the news in shock. So many people died, lost loved ones, and were displaced because of this natural disaster.

I wasn't a believer at the time, but Derek's dad was a pastor. When I told him to call his dad, he did.

"Why?" I challenged Tom. "If there is a God and He created everything, then why would He do *this*?" I didn't mean only what happened in Japan. If there was a God, I was mad at Him because He didn't protect people, including me. "Why would God allow all these people to die?"

I will never forget Tom's answer. It didn't make me become a Christian or soften what I saw on the news, but his answer planted a seed.

"Ashley," Tom said, "I do not have an answer for you except that there is good and there is evil, and if there wasn't evil, sadness, and heartbreak, then we could never appreciate the good."

Okay, I thought. That answer sufficed.

***

One night Derek and I went to a club with five or six of his football buddies. We must have had fake IDs, but I can't say for certain; my memory of this night is foggy. Derek and his friends were huge—we're talking about big boys. I was well protected that night, but my vices still got the better of me.

I'd been drinking, and for some reason, I decided to leave the club. I had a bunch of washed bills in my Louis Vuitton clutch. Fake twenties and hundreds. Just because I'd left California did not mean I was now a new person. I had no intention of changing *me*. I just wanted a change of scenery.

I decided to share a cab with some college students. Or people I thought were college students because we were close to a university. Whether it was the liquid courage or plain ol' poor decision-making, I thought sharing a cab with people I had just met was a fine choice.

The next thing I knew, a red car pulled up next to us. Men grabbed me, shoved me inside the car, and took me to a filthy motel. I remember being "helped" through a lobby toward a room where the carpet was all pulled up and three men were digging a hole in the ground. The sight made my skin crawl. Adrenaline coursed through me, and although I didn't believe in God, my spirit wrestled inside me and I *knew* something evil and dark was going on. I froze on the inside, but on the outside, I started yelling and kicking and displaying all this newfound courage—I did not want to go *in there*. I must have caused a big enough scene because they took me to a different room, where I was drugged and then gang raped.

I was in and out of consciousness, but I remember seeing many men and I knew they were operating multiple rooms, each one with a girl inside.

I don't know if I was in that motel room for hours or days. Many people passed in and out, and I assume these men were selling drugs, not just running girls. They kept me pretty drugged up, which in hindsight I am thankful for. I cannot imagine what it would have been like to experience that room sober. By this point, my body and brain were used to being numb. I knew these men were running girls across state lines because I overheard conversations about where they were going that night. Talk about Arkansas, Illinois, Kansas, and Tennessee echoed in the rooms.

I had no phone; they had taken it the moment they shoved me into the car. They also had my clutch with all the washed money. Probably assuming it was real. I'd never heard the words *human trafficking*, but I did, of course, know there was a market for sex. Just that week I'd been looking for jobs in strip clubs, lingerie shops, gentlemen's bars, and the like. Everything Rory had taught me still lived in my head. That's the power of a trauma bond. I believed that my only future, all I would ever become, somehow involved sex. This situation was no exception. Rory's words ached inside me.

Eventually I found myself sitting on a disgusting bed and wearing nothing but an oversized t-shirt that didn't belong to me. As I stared up at the stained ceiling, I began to cry. Crying was not something I did often, especially when my emotions were masked by chemicals, but I remember just giving up. Crying meant I had surrendered to the probability that I was just about to be transported to another state and never found. As I wept, I beat myself up for all the decisions that had led me to this point.

Everything after this moment happened so fast that even as I write the story now, I can feel my heart pounding behind my ribs.

I realized I was in the room alone. The tears stopped. Heart thundering, I jumped up from the bed and began searching through all the drawers until I found it.

My phone.

***

The day before this incident, I had been in Springfield with Derek and his friends. We visited an apartment where some Missouri State guys lived. I think the purpose of this visit was to grab some weed, but I was just along for the ride. Derek's phone died, and he used mine to let one of the guys know we were downstairs.

That phone call saved my life. I was too fearful and ashamed to call Derek. Our history was complicated enough, and in that moment of panic and rash decision-making, I didn't call him. Instead, I called Trey, the guy Derek had used my phone to call.

When Trey answered, the words just spilled out of me. "I know you don't know me, but I was at your apartment the other day…" I didn't even know where I was now. I scanned the room for the name of the motel. The room had a useless phone—the wires had been cut—but the name of the motel was printed on the bottom. I hurriedly told Trey the motel's name and asked if he could look up the address, knowing that at any moment, somebody could walk back into the room and my plan would be over.

We hung up.

And I waited.

***

When I tell this story to an audience, I usually skip most of the details and arrive at the fact that a stranger's kindness rescued me. While that is true for time's sake, there is also so much more to this part of the story. So much of God's unmeasurable goodness woven in, His remarkable pursuit of me. I don't know why *I* was rescued that day over any other girl locked in that motel. I don't know what caused my abusers to leave for those crucial ten minutes. I don't know why Trey answered his phone or why he and his two roommates decided to come get me.

But they did.

And I don't want to think about where I would be if they hadn't.

They came barging into the room, scooped me up, and said, "Let's go." Walked me to their car. Didn't bat an eye at any of the guys standing outside the rooms.

They drove me back to their apartment, and no one said a word to me on the drive. And for that, I was thankful—I didn't have words, and the shame drenched me like water. Part of me thought that no one would believe me, and another part thought, *This is just what happens to girls like me.*

Trey offered me his room, a shower, and some clothes. I slept for a few hours, so thankful for the absence of questions, for the absence of words. As much as I didn't have answers, those guys probably didn't know what to say either. They didn't want to ask questions. They were college athletes, not keen on seedy motel rooms or the world of methamphetamine or trafficking operations. They just accepted the fact I was in trouble and helped me. A complete stranger.

One of Trey's roommates drove me back to the two-bedroom apartment I had rented weeks earlier. Derek was waiting for me when I arrived. He'd probably been there for hours. He had called my mom because nobody knew where I was, and he didn't know what to do.

Now that I stood in front of him, how in the world was I supposed to explain what happened? I couldn't look him in the eye. There were so many things I could have said, but my explanation seemed too grand to deliver right then. So I was silent. He probably assumed I went home with somebody else or left in search of hard drugs—any of the things I had done before. Like I said, our history was colorful, and I don't blame him for what might have run through his mind.

In the end, I don't think we spoke. The silence spoke more loudly, and the room filled with heavy sadness. Disappointment flooded his eyes, and I wondered if he could feel the guilt seeping out of my pores. I felt dirty and questioned if what I had experienced was even real. Did that *really* happen? Again, I felt nobody would believe me.

CHAPTER 5

Derek eventually left. The door closed with what felt like finality.

***

I am a runner. When things go south, I feel like I failed and I want to start over. I have this tick inside me, this flick of bravery that, at any moment, allows me to pick up and move to a new place. Even today, healed and healthy, if somebody said, "Let's move to New York," I would say, "Great! Let's go." And I would.

I knew I didn't want to go home to California. I had just made this massive move across the country, and I couldn't admit defeat so quickly. Maybe I had something to prove to my parents. Or maybe to myself. But I just kept running, farther and farther away.

I really, really wanted to get high. When I decided to move to Missouri, I stopped doing meth. I knew Derek would be able to tell the minute I got there if I was high, so I refrained. In the absence of meth, I had put on some weight and was looking healthy. Besides drinking occasionally with Derek and his friends, I was staying clean.

But what happened in the motel room activated my addiction. Not only did they give me drugs, but now, after the comedown, I felt I needed something to help me numb out, to get what I had just experienced out of my head. Thankfully, the person I was before coming to Missouri was sneaky, deceitful, and proactive. "I should probably bring some dope with me *just in case*." I had not prepared for *this* just-in-case scenario, of course, but I'd brought one small bag of meth with me, zipped in a jacket pocket packed in my suitcase. I spent the next few days wired in my apartment. Alone.

51

What I chose to do next was bizarre and speaks to my desperate need for validation. I began contacting people I hadn't spoken to in years. Female friends who didn't seem to hate me. Any guy I used to have a romantic interest in—men I'd never dated or been in a relationship with, but at one point, we were mutually attracted to one another. I began writing them on Facebook, seeing where I could move next. Southern California, Pennsylvania, Oregon, and—my last choice—back home.

When I was sober in Southern California, I had lived with a ton of awesome girls who were also in recovery. One of them in particular went through rehab and sober living with me, and we'd gotten an apartment together. Her name was Emma. In my loneliness and the search for a new place, I reached out to her and she answered the call.

"I don't live in SoCal anymore," she told me. "I'm in Georgia. This is where I'm from."

I hadn't told many people about what happened to me, but I did tell her, and she dropped everything to drive from Georgia to Missouri to get me.

Looking back at that act of pure love, I think what meant the most to me was that she *believed* me. She believed what I said had happened. Many survivors don't speak up because they are afraid nobody will listen. But Emma did.

She drove twenty-four hours across multiple state lines to find me completely twacked out of my mind. Scared, high, anxious, and wearing the most ridiculous outfit. I don't remember any of our conversations when she arrived or if we derived a plan; all I recall is wanting to go to Walmart at 3:00 a.m. (Classic tweaker behavior. If you know, you know.)

CHAPTER 5

"Why do people who do meth feel the need to wear all their favorite clothes?" Emma asked in a passive-aggressive tone. Polite, but clearly suggesting I needed to change. "Your favorite hat, your favorite boots, those sparkly pants, and the vintage tee are all fine by themselves, but they do not need to be worn together. At the same time."

In all my drug-induced tweaker glory, I was royally offended that my beanie with the pom-pom didn't go with my spaghetti-strap tank top and fur boots in twenty-degree weather. But I considered her suggestion. She did drive all this way.

Somewhere between Walmart and the next morning, I left Missouri. I don't think I ever said goodbye to Derek. I just wanted to escape. Shame poured through me so hard that I reverted to the only thing I knew how to do in order to cope: get high.

Emma drove another twenty-four hours to Georgia. And what did *I* do on the trip? I took ten thousand pictures of myself.

We crossed through Kentucky, Tennessee, and finally entered Georgia, pulling up in a suburban neighborhood. As I stepped onto that red Georgia clay, the thick humidity hit me, and I felt like I couldn't breathe. It wasn't even summer yet! I had lived at sea level my whole life, and I realized then how spoiled I was.

***

Emma let me stay with her, but I could sleep on her floor for only so long before the urge to explore gripped me. I wanted to get out and meet new people.

But for the first time in my life, raw, unexpected fear made this difficult. It was far easier to trust the people *she* introduced me to, so I began hanging out with one of her childhood friends. His name was Dustin. One day he took me to Trader Joe's to grab a job application, and then he asked, "Do you want to go get some coke?"

Yes. I did.

He drove us to the Bluff, an area of Atlanta commonly referred to as Zone 6, where you can get pretty much anything you want. Drugs, guns, girls. It was not safe, and we stood out like a sore thumb. I was smoking a cigarette with my window down when about ten guys swarmed the car.

"Lemme buy that girl! Lemme buy that girl" they shouted. "Sell me that girl, man!"

I locked eyes with Dustin, confused. "Do you sell coke? I thought that's what we came here to get." I thought they were referring to "white girl," another name for cocaine.

"They're talking about *you*," he said quickly in his southern drawl. "Roll your window up."

I sat with those words for a minute. I guess some part of me thought Georgia would be different. New territory, new people. But no.

Why was it that everywhere I went, men thought I was for sale?

***

Eventually I got my act together. I left the comfort of Emma's apartment and moved out on my own. I started working at Trader Joe's, and my mom came to visit. Things began to settle in, and I felt a spirit of newness coming. This was good, wasn't it? This move across the country had turned out okay after all. I told myself I could do this. "I can make it on my own."

I still had trouble trusting people because of what happened in Missouri. My coworkers were awesome and tried hard to get to know me. They invited me to parties and out to dinner, but I felt uncomfortable in my own skin. I wasn't using or drinking, and I was very lonely. Shortly after moving out of Emma's apartment, I cut ties with her, severing my relationship with the only person I truly knew in Georgia. Every time I got to know somebody else, I began to question their character. It seemed like I didn't have the ability to discern or judge if they were safe or not, so I stopped trying to get to know people altogether. In an attempt to compartmentalize my life, I didn't want anybody to know where I lived. Work, home, dinner, sleep, repeat. That cycle felt safe.

One day at work, I stepped outside to take my break when two regulars approached me. After some small talk, Matt and his brother handed me a business card and asked, "Would you be interested in a second job?"

The card read DIAMOND's in pretty script.

"You'll have to get an alcohol permit because you aren't twenty-one yet," Matt said.

"Okay, I'll think about it," I replied.

"Yeah, think about it and let me know if you're interested. You'd make a lot of money!" He smiled as he walked away.

I could work both jobs—one in the day and the other at night. Save all my money, I thought. He hadn't asked for my number, and that gave the whole thing a sense of legitimacy. Plus I wanted the extra cash, and anything sounded better than feeling lonely and disconnected inside my apartment. So I took the bait.

Diamond's, in case you haven't guessed, was a gentleman's club. Matt's father owned it. True to his word, Matt took me to get my alcohol permit.

I hadn't encountered anyone in Georgia who did meth yet, and it was as if that darkness lay dormant in me, waiting for the moment when I would meet the monster again. Matt and his brothers were about my age, and they saw right away that I didn't have any friends, so they began inviting me to family BBQs that I attended a few times to be polite.

"Have you ever used meth?" I casually asked Matt one day.

His ears got red as he looked at me sideways in the passenger seat. "Agh," he sighed, as if he knew he was about to disappoint me. How wrong he was. "Yes, I had a really bad problem with it back in the day."

I knew right then and there that I could find it if I wanted it.

In recovery, people often say that while you're getting sober, your disease is waiting, out there doing push-ups in the parking lot, and that's what it was like with me. I decided I was going to manipulate Matt. I think he had a crush on me, and I knew he would tell me where to go to get what I wanted.

***

I cocktail-waitressed at the club for two whole nights before one of the dancers with a thick Tennessee accent began taking shots of Jack Daniel's with me.

"Look at you," Tennessee exclaimed. "You should be up *there!*" She took me backstage and shoved a bikini at me. "Go dance, girl!"

Walking up to that stage for the first time was totally nerve racking. But it also did something for me. Working in the clubs gave me a false sense of power. It filled me with strength and gave me my confidence back, as I felt like I was taking from every man what he had stolen from me.

CHAPTER 5

I became very good at manipulating and made more money
than any other girl at the club. After all the times men had touched
me and I didn't want them to, now *I* was in control and got paid
for it.

However, I was running on fumes trying to maintain both
jobs. And both personas. One daytime persona and another at
night. I was working 6:00–3:00 at TJs and 6:00–3:00 at the club. I
crashed my new car after work one night about two minutes from
my apartment out of pure exhaustion and sleep deprivation. Matt
and his brother came to help me—I didn't have anybody else to
call, and the realization didn't sit well with me. Although I was
grateful for their help, they now knew where I lived, something
I'd managed to keep private since arriving in Georgia. But that
boundary came crumbling down.

***

One late afternoon, as Georgia's muggy weather formed sweat
beads on my neck, I walked in the front door of the club and
collided with a customer. I will never forget the way he looked
at me.

"Who are *you?*" he asked.

"I'm Ryann," I replied, using my new stripper name that felt
more like an alternate personality.

"You work night shift?"

"Yes," I said in a soft voice, slanting my eyes.

He turned right around and went back into the club to await
my shift.

The nights Hank came to the club, I always felt conflicted. I
knew I had a chance to make more money than usual, but there

57

was something inside me that wanted to scream, "No!" at the things he did. That part of me went silent as I purposefully bypassed myself to please him and walk away with more cash.

No amount of money is worth any of these memories, but I was so detached from my body that I just went through the motions. Low lighting. Music blasting. The faint smell of cigarettes lingering in the room. Hank would ask for a lap dance, sometimes paying me throughout my whole shift so I wouldn't go with another customer. The DJ would call me to the stage; I'd dance my two songs and return to Hank's section of the room. He liked that. That's what he wanted. He always positioned himself in the corner of the club, the darkest part of the room. I should have known better.

One night as I danced song after song, he suddenly pulled himself out and shoved me down on top of him. This wasn't a private room but the open floor. His boldness shocked me.

When I whipped my head around to say something, he held me down on top of him. "Just keep dancing," he said. "Everything's cool."

Except everything isn't cool, I thought. There was no request, no condom, and not to mention I could lose my job.

But Hank sold coke, which he generously served me for free. I began going to parties with him and some of the other girls a few nights a week. Until he stopped inviting them. He had horrible taste in music. He would take me to a hotel room, do some lines, throw some hundreds at me. Then while he raped me, I would focus on the lyrics playing in the background. "Five Star" by Yo Gotti, his favorite, would play over and over, and I began to loathe that song.

These were quick encounters. He would drop me off at my car, discard me promptly after he was finished. I questioned what

I was doing, but he had come to expect it, and I guess in a way so did I. When I saw him walk into the club, I knew what time it was.

***

One night when my shift ended, I cashed out, tipped out, and breathalyzed. As a bouncer walked me to my car, I saw Hank waiting. We were not allowed to leave with customers, so I knew to meet him at his hotel.

When I arrived, he said, "Get in the car. I want to take you somewhere different tonight."

I can't say I "enjoyed" going to unsafe places, but as we drove down Fulton Industrial Boulevard, the danger began to call to me. My legs were shaking the way they often did when I was threatened, but excitement rose in my chest. This was the trauma speaking; I just didn't know her name yet. The high highs and low lows, knowing something was about to happen. Survival mode flipped on, adrenaline running through my veins.

We pulled up to another strip club, and I looked around in confusion. I didn't want to go in there.

"I just came from work!" I whined.

He told me to hush as the valet showed him where to park, and we were let in through a side entrance. I remember feeling curious about why we didn't use the front door, and I supposed it was either because I wasn't twenty-one yet or because Hank had a gun. As I walked in, I recognized the place, although I had never been there before. All strip clubs have the same feel. The same smell—stale sweetness—and the rainbow club lighting. I noticed I was the only white girl in the room. Hank whispered to people as we passed by.

That night I met Dante.

This was a different type of exploitation. I never thought of Hank as my pimp or that he "owned" me in any way. He would just show up at my job every so often, and I knew those nights were "his." He was my highest paying customer, but as I walked behind him at this new club, I watched as an exchange happened between him and Dante. He had "sold" me—inadvertently, because I didn't belong to anybody.

But that was the last time I saw Hank. And the beginning of Dante contacting me.

CHAPTER 6

*Consciously, I was choosing a life that made sense only to me,
instead of choosing something that would give me refuge.
Freedom versus safety—there seemed no way to have both.*

—CARISSA PHELPS, *RUNAWAY GIRL*

Strange things happened to me again and again due to my being spun out and hanging around certain people. I never stayed in one place too long. I was unpredictable and delusional. But again, in an odd way, it feels to me like meth saved me.

"Get off the drugs," Dante said. "I see so much potential in you."

Yeah, potential for him to make money, but he couldn't when I was that high.

I began to suffer from identity disturbance. I was Ashley... but more often I was Ryann. I was Ryann more because I was working more. Ryann made it easier for Ashley to cope with the profession she had landed in. So there was a duality surrounding my identity, and who I was felt distorted. I knew I had to abandon Ashley in order to embody Ryann. Ryann was easier, so I began being her all the time. She was braver, she masked emotion, she was able to perform, and she was able to do things Ashley was uncomfortable with. I became lost within this character I created for myself. Ryann was reckless. But Ryann also felt safe.

Dante and another guy kept trying to get me to "work" for them. They invited me different places that always turned out to be sex parties. I frequently saw girls getting trains run on them (essentially gang raped), and I was surrounded by people smoking crack.

But the meth set me apart and made me undesirable. My skin was picked all over; I was tweaking, sketchy, twitchy.

As strange as it sounds, I see the hand of God in all of these events. I know they are not easy to read about, to digest the idea that this is somehow "normal" in today's world, yet for me personally, things could have easily turned out much worse than they did. It's possible I might not have been allowed to leave. I could have been fully immersed in the control of these men I was meeting at the clubs, yet something protected me. Some invisible shield seemed to hover over me in dangerous places with dangerous people, even when I kept making unwise decisions.

Interestingly, as I became Ryann more and more frequently, my ex-trafficker Rory was checking my voicemail messages. Remember when voicemail had a special pin code? He, for whatever reason, began checking up on me again and he quickly put two and two together, and he began listening to messages that customers left for me on my phone. He called my mom and told her I was stripping or sleeping with guys for money. (He wasn't sure which.)

But I was a good liar. Quick and prepared. When my mother called me, I reminded her that he was crazy, which he was. I still don't understand what he thought he would get out of that phone call. That my mom would be so thankful for his concerned citizenship that she would just hand me over to him? Funny how he, out of all people, was "concerned" for my safety. He laid the foundation for where I now stood.

***

On the nights I wasn't working, I did meth.

Matt, who had recruited me to his father's strip club, was my only connection to the meth world and the first person to shoot me up. In his defense, I begged him to. I'd shot heroin before but not meth, and I needed his help. *That* feeling—the rush of warmth, the tingling hyper-awareness of all of the senses, that first-time feeling—is the high I began chasing. Matt wanted me to keep working at his dad's club, so it was an easy exchange to convince him to take me to get some dope.

When he pulled into a trailer park in Acworth, I felt a ball of nerves in my stomach. As stereotypical as this sounds, I pictured all the movies, people, and drugs that talked about the exact place I now found myself in. I'd never set foot in a trailer park. First time for everything, right? As anxiety coursed through me, I also felt excitement, anticipation. A feeling I always got right before I picked up.

I met a lot of people that day, including a girl my age who "rented a room" inside the trailer we were visiting; a guy who called himself Bam Bam and told me I looked like a mixture of Amy Winehouse and Lady Gaga; and Kam, who was outside working on his truck.

I was never attracted to Matt, but he had some strange possessiveness over me. Especially at work. People began to think we were together, which I *hated* and he apparently didn't.

He started showing up at my apartment unannounced, and he always went on these long rants about how much he wanted to be with me, take care of me. I was not interested. I didn't want to be around him a minute longer.

But standing there talking to Kam, I felt an instant connection. My entire being knew I shouldn't be there in a trailer park, yet I would go anywhere if it meant I got to stand next to this guy. This stranger. Paradoxically, I felt safe. A feeling I hadn't felt in a long time.

"Do you live here?" I asked him.

He laughed, flashing a perfect smile. "In the trailer park? Naw, I don't."

"Let's get out of here then," I responded. No hesitation. Just take me with you. Now.

***

How we envision these things going and how they *actually* go are usually two different pictures.

I felt my body calm the minute we stepped into Kam's house. Yet it wasn't exactly *his* house. As I found out later, it was the mother of his daughter's house, who did not do drugs and worked full time. I quickly learned that his drug use was the source of their problems. So he spent most of his time in Canton at his uncle's house, and his daughter's mom spent her time working and raising their kid. Red flags, anyone? Regardless, I spent all my time with him.

We became close. I was around him and his uncle John every single waking second, and I fell in love with his then two-year-old daughter, Tristan. Yes, Kam and his uncle partied, but they also took me in as family, something I hadn't found since touching down in Georgia. They were the first people I began to trust, and I fell hard for Kam. Our connection was like that of an affair. Emotional intensity, lust masked as love, fierce attraction, and consuming chemistry—yet he was also unavailable. Noncommittal and sneaky. He would take off for days at a time, not to go "home" to his daughter's mom, but to other girls. This crushed me, and at the same time, all I wanted was just to be near him.

In fact, I wanted to be near him so badly that I willingly traded my new, fully furnished apartment for a pop-up camper on Kam's uncle's property in the boonies. I didn't sleep, so the camper was just a place where I could get high and change my clothes. It served its purpose, or so I thought, but in all honesty, only somebody on meth would ever have found this situation acceptable. I kept most of my belongings at the apartment I was renting out; I would shower there and get ready at the club on the nights I worked. The camper had no running water or bathroom, so I would pee in large cups from gas stations and have to dump them outside. I would come home from work at 3:00 or 4:00 in the morning to centipedes crawling on the wall. Darkness surrounded me.

I was in love with Kam, and he knew it. Sleeping together was my first mistake. Before I knew it, I was paying his probation fees, buying him dope, and watching his daughter whenever he needed help. He would take off to run mystery errands and leave me with Tristan. Regardless of how much her father drove me utterly insane, I became very attached to this little girl. I loved her and felt like she was the one spark of light in my sunless world.

One night I went to my apartment to shower and couldn't get the door open. Somebody had replaced the locks. I managed to get in through the sliding glass door and discovered that everything I owned was gone. My clothes, my computer, my TV, my furniture. The place was empty.

My renters and I did drugs; that was the only way we knew each other and the only logical reason I had let a fifty-year-old man live in my apartment with his girlfriend. To this day, I have no idea why they robbed me—what rumor or misguided information they thought they had on me that pushed them to retaliate. I chalked it up to yet another symptom of the Georgia drug game. Befriend people in order to rob them. It was a common theme that, unfortunately, I experienced more than once. I learned a hard lesson through it.

Eventually I got evicted from that apartment, and I started working more since I had just lost everything. Kam knew I couldn't keep living out of that camper. Maybe he felt guilty because he knew I had exchanged my comfort to be closer to him and then got robbed. So he offered me the guest room at his baby mama's house.

That was when I finally met Chrissy. She was so normal and I was not. Though she kept me at a distance and was obviously skeptical, I realized she was welcoming me in her own way. There was a willingness in her to help me. On the many nights when Kam was off doing God knows what, I was at home with Chrissy and Tristan. She had to have known about the drugs, and what Kam and I were doing ate me alive, but she and I were cool, partly because she knew I loved her daughter.

***

I ended up quitting Diamond's to get away from Matt, and I worked at five different strip clubs during my time in Georgia. As I walked away from the first club, I learned the grass *was* greener on the other side. The high ceilings of Mardi Gras Gentlemen's Club called my name.

While I worked, I often let Kam take my car. He'd drop me off and some nights forget to pick me back up. Other nights he would show up on time, only to immediately ask how much money I'd made. I would hand it over, and he would buy dope or just take the money for himself. In the process of writing this book, I realized he qualifies as another abuser in my story. I romanticized him for years, even still held love for him, instead of seeing the situation for what it truly was: coercion.

Kam's uncle adored me when we first met. He would say things like, "I am on your team, babygirl. I am for you."

And I made a discovery, or thought I did. *All these people are good down in their core. It's the drugs that make them do bad things.* I always wondered what people would be like without the drugs. Uncle John was no exception to this observation; he was completely for me—unless he was for himself, and then I was disposable.

John began introducing me to his "friends." On the days we couldn't find any dope, John would casually mention that he had a friend he wanted me to meet. These old countrymen would show up, or I would go meet them at hotel rooms. I knew what it was without anybody saying anything. I got what I wanted out of the exchange, and so did they.

The only thing I cared about was sticking a needle in my arm. The funny part is I couldn't do it myself. I refused to get high any other way, so I had to find people who would help me. This gave John and other men an "in" with me. It exposed a vulnerability I had, and John in particular used it to his advantage. I didn't want to do what they wanted—but I wanted the needle more, so I allowed these encounters. I never would have let them touch me, come into my space, without this raging desire for the high.

***

One summer evening, I became extremely ill and thought the only thing that would make me feel better was a shot of dope. And it did. The adrenaline kicked in and gave my body a false boost. The aches disappeared for a while as I rode the wave. I don't know how many days I remained in this state before Kam and his uncle finally took me to the hospital. I vaguely remember eating a PB&J sandwich and different nurses coming in and asking the same questions.

"You have MRSA," someone told me. A staph infection that is highly resistant to antibiotics.

I couldn't go back to work at the club for a little while. With limited resources in Georgia and no family around, I did what I could while relying on my best judgment, which was, of course, clouded by drugs. I chose to "trust" certain people who seemed like they could help me—even after they did things like abuse me or rob my apartment. But it wasn't so much about trust as it was manipulation. I was looking out for myself, or so I believed, and if these people had drugs, I sought them. If they could shoot me up, I sought them. If I needed a place to stay for the night, I sought them.

That is how I ended up in a nasty motel room with Ron, the old man who had rented my apartment and then robbed me blind. I needed what he had, and I knew just how to get it—all I had to do was bypass my intuition and float away from my body. His piercing blue eyes are burned into my memory. A wave of stomach bile rises at the back of my throat when I think of them. We would do a shot, and immediately he would want what he came for. This used to make me so mad—I just wanted to feel my high, to chill for a second. Instead, I had to feel somebody else, to please *him*.

During encounters like these, I began to disassociate. The best way to describe it is that I watched myself from above. I was another entity watching myself perform sexual acts. Or sometimes I would settle into a sea of utter stillness, enveloped by pitch black. When it was over, I would come back, stepping into reality again. This particular night as Ron grabbed me, I settled into darkness.

***

Throughout this season, I questioned God's existence time and time again, but I can see now that He *was* there. I just didn't understand the extent of my free will. I thought God was an entity that controlled the outcome, and I blamed His lack of involvement for everything wrong with the world. Yet God is the opposite of controlling. He is an observer, a creator, *and* an author of our stories, but He is also loving. He is not intrusive; He lets us walk our own way, even if we change the narrative and take the hard road instead of the path He carved out for us. That is love.

But sometimes He does intervene. Like He did that night with Ron.

Someone knocked on the door.

Why were the cops here? It made no sense, other than the fact that I was with a sketchy guy, in a sketchy motel room, doing sketchy drugs. I had dope in a zippered pouch hanging in a bag in the closet, and as they took Ron out of the room to question him, a young cop searched the drawers, under the mattress, looking for dope or paraphernalia. He opened the door to the closet, saw my bags in there—and shut the door without checking them.

I remember sitting on the bed trembling, half dressed in an oversized, long-sleeve shirt.

"What are you doing here?" the cop asked.

I had no answer.

He sighed and said, "Let me see your arms."

I pulled up my left sleeve and showed him skin covered in tattoos. The other arm I left mostly concealed, trying to hide my track marks. I felt my face flood with shame.

The officer had kind eyes as he looked at me and said, "I don't know what you're doing here, especially with *him*, but I suggest you take all your stuff out of here and get as far away from him as you possibly can."

A warning. That was all it was.

The night was unexplainable. They didn't find the dope, I didn't get arrested, and Ron was nowhere to be found. He just vanished into thin air. Following the officer's advice, I packed my things and left the room deserted.

***

It seemed like everyone who did drugs in the Atlanta area eventually crossed paths with each other. I saw this strange interconnectedness as relationships and people overlapped.

One night I met a girl named Shelly. Engaging in my normal after-work, middle-of-the-night activities, I had just finished getting high with a friend when I jumped on the back of his street bike and we ended up at Shelly's hotel suite.

She was *not* pleased that we were there. Ignoring my presence completely, she said to my friend Andrew, "Thanks for the heads-up that you were bringing company. What do you need?"

70

CHAPTER 6

"Oh, Ashley?" he said. "She's cool."

"So I've *heard*," Shelly replied snarkily.

I wondered what she'd heard about me.

"Don't act like that—and I need a half," Andrew said.

Shelly and Andrew went into the other room and closed the door. I could tell she didn't trust me and didn't want me to have any evidence that she sold dope—even though I was about to leave with the guy she just gave a half-pound to. Regardless, I sat on the couch and waited for them, rummaging through my purse, organizing, acting like I also had something to do.

Shelly suddenly swept back into the room like a whirlwind, yelling about some of her clothes going missing. I stared at her blankly as she searched through her things and looked at me suspiciously out the corner of her eye.

I realized what this was. "Look," I said. "While I was waiting for y'all, I promise I didn't steal any of your things."

I stood up, took my purse, and proceeded to dump the entire thing on the floor in front of her. I guess we both were used to people always wanting something from us. I came to learn that Shelly wasn't just a dope girl—she was *the* dope girl. And apparently didn't have many female friends. In one moment, I proved my loyalty.

I was not a drug dealer at the time but a drug user. Shelly knew that. I guess that's another reason she began to trust me—I wasn't competition, I had no agenda, and I danced, so I had my own money. A group of Shelly's guy friends frequented the club, and I slowly started to meet them.

One day Shelly and I walked into the guys' house, and Corey looked at her in surprise and joked, "*You* have a friend?"

"Yes," Shelly replied with a sassy undertone. "Not that it's any of your business, but I really like Ashley."

"Oh yeah? But which Ashley have you met? She has about seven personalities."

Corey and I had crossed paths a few times; he was trying to be funny, but he was exposing my crazy.

There was a love triangle going on between Shelly and two of the guys, but it was none of my business. I just knew she supplied the house with dope, and everyone living there sold drugs and had their own clientele. They often frequented the club where I worked, and their house was much closer than mine, so on the nights I drank too much or didn't feel like making the drive home, I would stop by Corey and Nick's. Many times I had been awake for days and ended up falling asleep on their couch. They never tried to sleep with me or rob me. In fact, multiple times I woke up in the morning to find that they had put all my earnings from the night before in their safe. They looked out for me, and I felt like I was beginning to have "friends."

***

The holidays were here, and my family expected me home for Christmas. I arrived at the airport early, with enough time to take a bunch of muscle relaxers with a friend. We sat in the airport together...without actually going *into* the terminal. I was so messed up on Somas that by the time I realized I needed to get to security, I missed my flight.

My mom was furious. "It's Christmas Eve! They are going to charge me $900 for a new ticket!" She protested—but then did it anyway.

I made it home, and my mom could immediately tell I was unwell. I'd brought dope and pills with me on the plane, managing to walk through the body scan machine with drugs hidden in my bra—I have no idea how I got away with that. Again, it was protection I didn't deserve from a God I didn't know. My mom was tired of my lies. She wanted the truth about my life in Georgia, and when she laid eyes on me, I confirmed her suspicions.

My mom became very sneaky over the years. She had to, since I could not tell her the truth. She didn't even bother asking me to be honest anymore because everything that came out of my mouth was a bald-faced lie. I was living a double life; add substances to that equation, and it was hard for me to keep up with all of my stories.

My mom and I conveniently had the same kind of phone. While I was in the shower one night, she switched them. I hate that I had completely shattered her trust that she felt she needed to do things like this.

"Sorry, I thought this was my phone," she said, sliding my phone back to me as if it were an accident.

I stood there, my hair wrapped in a towel, and stared at her. When I checked my phone, I saw she had Googled the name of the club where I worked. The internet describes it as a "gentleman's club," but my mom isn't stupid. This was not the first time she suspected I was working in the commercial sex industry. If only she knew that my job at a strip club was the least of her worries.

For a long time, I resented my mom for invading my privacy, not just with this incident but for the majority of my life. However, I gave her a reason to and I see that now. She was so scared. Instead of focusing on Christmas Eve dinner with our family, she had to play detective, worried sick about me and my safety. We didn't enjoy the time we had together. I sneaked around trying to get high for the three days I was home, while she sneaked around trying to find out the truth about my life back in Georgia. I couldn't wait to leave, and she couldn't hold on tightly enough.

When I got home from California, I didn't bat an eye—I went right back to work at the club, partying hard and surrounding myself with my newfound "friends."

***

One random Tuesday night, I got fired from Mardi Gras. I wasn't even planning on going to work that night, but I was rolling on ecstasy and thought, *Why not go make some money?* Another dancer reported that her wallet had gone missing, and the staff began searching the dressing room, checking lockers and bags.

I didn't care about the wallet. I hadn't stolen anything, but I was worried about the contents of my bag. As they opened my locker and started going through makeup bags and zippered pouches, the house mom looked startled.

"Oh wow," she said as she unzipped a bag with dope, pills, and a syringe. "Whose locker is this?"

I stepped forward, trying to appear more sober than I was.

"You're fired," she said, and as I protested, she put the drugs in her pocket. "You'll be escorted out."

"So I'm getting fired *and* you're keeping what you found?" I replied with attitude, knowing damn well she wasn't going to turn anything in but use them herself.

"I'm keeping these, or I can call the police. Which do you choose?"

She had me.

CHAPTER 6

As the valet pulled my car to the door, I felt embarrassed. And livid. "Why did I even go to work on a slow-ass Tuesday night!?" Looking for someone to blame. Like it was Tuesday's fault.

***

A short time later, I went to see Shelly at her apartment, and something was off. She was talking about the police watching her—it was like she knew her time was running out.

Sitting with her on her bed, I listened as she told me what to do in case something happened that night. Hearing her desperation, I watched my sweet friend and just soaked her in. She gave me the code to the safe and I left, hoping deep down I wouldn't ever need to use it, that she was wrong and I would see her the next day.

She got popped that night for the biggest bust in Cherokee County known to date. Before the cops arrived to raid her apartment, I headed that way and grabbed what dope she had left in the safe like we planned. I had just gotten fired, my best friend was arrested, and I was alone. There was no one to trust; everyone was a suspect, and now I had more drugs on me than even I felt comfortable with. I was freaked out. Paranoid. And knew I needed to lie low.

At this point, I was renting a room (literally sleeping on the floor) from a woman named Jan. After moving twelve times that year, I kept everything I owned in my car and stayed anywhere somebody would let me. Strange things happen when you do meth. The way I met Jan was strange, and she proved to be even stranger as time went on. It's like she was expecting me when I got there. She also claimed to have things of mine, like my birth certificate, passport, and all the other documents Ron stole out of my apartment. She was obviously unusual, but I also felt intrigued. I needed a place to stay, so I "bought" a room from her with dope. I didn't tell anybody I had everything Shelly left me. That sounded like an open invitation to rob me.

I hadn't seen Kam since I'd moved out of his baby mama's house and found my own group of friends, but I loved him or at least the idea of him; I loved our chemistry and kept selling myself false hope that one day it would work. So technically, he never *truly* left.

I decided to front Kam a half-ounce, thinking I could get a little bit of this weight off, and I knew he wouldn't try anything funny. It seemed like a safe choice. Who else could I count on in Georgia? The list kept getting smaller and smaller. So for whatever reason, I trusted him. Days later he made up some excuse about how he couldn't get the money.

"So where's the rest of the dope?" I challenged.

"I don't have it," he replied.

I just shook my head. I was tired of his games. All of them.

CHAPTER 7

I loved you at your darkest.

—ROMANS 5:8

I started working at a new club on FIB (Fulton Industrial Boulevard), the same street Hank took me to the night he "passed" me to Dante. The area is known for drugs, guns, exploitation, and grime, but I needed quick money, and I couldn't afford a permit to work at the better clubs.

I hated this club. Each night after I tipped out, I barely spoke to anyone, and the loneliness began to press down on me. I was practically homeless, my job was disgusting, and my best friend was in jail. I knew I needed to do something—find a new club, get out of Jan's house before I got bammed up, or she found all the dope I had stashed there. I needed one person I could trust. Just one.

I took a chance and called Nick. Corey's roommate and a friend of Shelly's.

***

That day I left work early because I felt like I had the flu. My entire body ached.

These guys from the club kept telling me about their "mansion" and how I should come home with them and party all weekend. I would rather have stuck my hand in a jar of razor blades. I was not interested.

If you have a mansion, I thought, *what the hell are you doing at* this *strip club? Better yet, why would you ever come down to Fulton Industrial Boulevard?*

But like a good girl, I refrained from being rude and politely declined their offer.

Sidenote—why do we do that as women? Worry so much about hurting the feelings of people we don't even know? For me, I know the answer: cultural conditioning. My family instilled in me as a child that young ladies are expected to be nice and polite at all costs. What this did was teach me to silence my own voice out of "politeness" (especially to please men) rather than speak my mind and listen to my intuition. I didn't get to *choose* if I wanted to give somebody a hug, shake their hand, or keep my mouth shut. It was just expected. This thought pattern was ingrained in me so severely that years later here I sat, in a strip club, choking out, "Thank you," in my most drippingly sweet tone to men who did not deserve such respect. Somehow what I learned as a child translated into *other* phrases too. Things that weren't good at all. *Bypass yourself, Sweetie. Give hugs even though you don't want to touch that person. Don't listen to your inner voice, Ash. Be "ladylike."*

These men were not being polite to me; they were being direct and forward. As soon as they saw me in a bikini, they wanted me to spend the night at their house. They didn't even know my name, but they liked my body so they made demands while I had to sit there and look pretty. I should have told them to fuck all the way off, but I didn't. I smiled and pacified them until I felt so violently ill that I had to leave work.

I was curled up in a ball on the floor when Nick got to my house.

"I don't know what's going on. I think I have the flu. I feel awful."

He sat with me and we talked. I told him about the night Shelly got arrested, how I had everything she left in her safe, and I was too scared to sell to anybody. I told him how much I missed my friend and how unsafe I felt at my job and my strange living arrangement with Jan. Everything felt off. Maybe I didn't have the flu. Maybe my nervous system was in a complete shutdown after being in constant overdrive day and night.

Nick and Jan knew each other from somewhere along the drug game. Throwing a giant freezer bag full of multicolored pills on top of Jan's bed, he asked her, "Need anything?"

They did their thing, and afterward he told her, "We'll be back."

He told me he would get the dope off for me. "You can come with me, so you know I'm not trying to do anything slick, and the money's yours too—I don't need it."

That's the kind of person Nick was. The entire time I knew him, he was forward, a little erratic from his time in the Army, but a good guy down to his core. He was a known pill man, but meth and pills usually go hand in hand.

"It's been super dry since Shelly got busted," he said, laughing to himself.

I guess *I* was the only one around with some dope, and I didn't know what to do with it.

"I want to introduce you to somebody," he said. "Come on."

***

We pulled up at a large house in a suburban neighborhood. Nick knocked on the door and walked inside without waiting for anyone to answer. Jessie was Nick's childhood friend. She and her husband, Doug, were functioning addicts. They both worked, lived in a beautiful home, and had kids together. Their son Luke was undiagnosed at the time, but I think he was autistic, and I fell in love with this special little boy. We had a bond—he's what sparked my desire to work with special needs kids. It didn't matter how buried I was in my drug addiction when it came to children.

Jessie welcomed me with open arms. I told her about the night before—the pompous men at work and my living situation on Jan's floor. She offered up her extra bedroom to me so I could rest. I ended up falling asleep right there on the bed next to her and Nick. As I drifted off, I could hear him sharing some of my story with her, and what he said was accurate. It felt good to hear somebody else say it outloud, and my body finally gave in to the weight of sleep.

When I woke up, all of us got high together and talked for hours like most people on drugs do.

"You could stay here if you want," Jessie offered. "You know, permanently."

"Really?" I asked, slightly disbelieving. Technically, we had just met. "Are you sure?"

She nodded.

CHAPTER 7

So I moved out of Jan's and into Jessie's. I rode around all day and night with Nick. He was a one-man show, but I watched and learned his mannerisms. Based on how he interacted with customers, I could tell if he trusted them or not. Some were friends; some were strictly business. We went county to county, and I learned the roads and my surroundings fairly quickly. Naturally, although I'm not exactly sure *when* it happened, I became Nick's girlfriend.

One day Nick looked over at me and said, "I want you to stop dancing."

It was still early in our relationship, and I remember the conversation vividly. He was gentle at first, trying to establish more understanding as he said, "I mean, do you like it? Working there?"

I explained how working in the strip clubs had given me something back, something I had lost in Missouri. Dancing filled me with confidence and allowed me to adopt a persona I was never brave enough to be without a stage. "But as of late, I hate it."

"I hear you," Nick said, "but I would never want somebody I'm dating, the person I'm committed to, to take their clothes off for money. I got you, girl. You don't have to do that anymore."

But I had a hard time letting go of my independence. Even after that conversation, I went back to the club a few more times. The thought of having my *own* money that *I* earned. Nick was not manipulative or controlling—he was right. I had everything I wanted. Money was not an issue, and the money was *ours*. We both had access to it. I just had a hard time shaking what my past had ingrained in me. I didn't want Nick to leave and for me to be stuck with nothing. I didn't want to rely on a man, and I wasn't fully convinced that Nick actually meant what he said. That I didn't *need* to dance.

My new identity had formed in the low lighting of a strip club. If I no longer needed to dance, what was I supposed to do? Who was I supposed to be?

**

Since I now had a boyfriend, this caused some tension between Kam and me. He would come around only when he was trying to buy dope, and the conversation usually turned sour.

"Really? You're just gonna go date this guy? Is that what you really want?" And in a jealous rage, he would storm off.

I know his jealousy was more about control than any real feelings he held for me. We had never truly "dated." I was always a secret—one of many secrets he kept from his daughter's mom. I can recognize now that he was just mad he no longer had me in his grasp, under his emotionally abusive snare.

The "family" Uncle John promised me had automatically disappeared when I stepped into a relationship with Nick. One day I planned to meet with George, one of Kam's cousins. He was also a pill guy, so Nick and I drove up there to meet him. George told me to meet him at the top of the hill—a place I'd never been. Kam had never *allowed* me to go up there, and I should have known better.

We pulled up, and George and a guy the size of a linebacker climbed into the back of my car. Nick went to exchange what we came for, and *click*. Gun cocked to the back of my head.

"You're gonna shoot me?" I screamed at George while his friend held the pistol firmly in place.

"Gimme the pills!" George shouted in a raspy voice. "Give 'em to me!"

CHAPTER 7

Nick was smart. He reached down carefully and grabbed off the floorboard what was maybe a half-ounce of weed and a little teenager bag of dope wrapped up for somebody else. He switched the giant pill bag worth well over five grand for this comparatively worthless package and threw it at George. Both guys scrambled out of my car and started running.

As I sat frozen in the driver's seat, Nick yelled, "Let's go, let's go, let's fucking go!" He turned bright red, slamming his fists on the dashboard.

I got my bearings and got us out of there. As I drove, I left screaming voicemails for every single person I knew who was related to Kam. My supposed "family" had just robbed me with a loaded gun to my head.

It felt good knowing they'd gotten us for a measly $150 and not one pill was in their hand. But Nick was furious.

I felt defeated.

***

Life with Nick was a whirlwind. We were constantly on the go, sleeping infrequently and selling drugs out of my car from sunrise to sunset. I observed and eventually immersed myself in this lifestyle, and I adopted another persona. A new one. This was a version of Ryann from the club, but this time I was untouchable. Nick and I drove all over the greater Atlanta area with a car full of drugs and guns. He had two cell phones and used to wear a bulletproof vest everywhere we went. I never thought, *Hey, do I need one of those? Is somebody really going to shoot us?* I just accepted what my life looked like and started carrying a Glock 19 in my purse. I lived in go mode, with my foot on the gas.

We sold practically every drug in existence. If somebody had it, Nick bought it and flipped it. We would drive people to doctor appointments. Pill Mills, as they are often called. Nick would pay for their visit and buy up all the pills the doctors prescribed. Patients would walk out of monthly appointments with prescriptions for 250 Xanax, 100 Oxicotin, 100 muscle relaxers every month for pain management, and Nick would buy them all. We were taking fifteen people to the doctor each month and stocking up on meth, mushrooms, and anything else we could get our hands on. We were a mobile narcotic candy store.

We stayed at Jessie's most of the time, but one month we rented a room from some young kids who grew weed in the basement. I used to call this house the drive-through pharmacy because people could pull into the first driveway and leave out the second. How great would it be to install a bucket levy system? If we had one of those, I could just drop pills through the second window.

But then one day the police went through our trash, and Nick and I were gone by the next morning. We never stayed in one place too long. We were reckless and wild, and so were all of our friends. Though we ran into the police many times, for whatever reason, nothing happened. It just wasn't our time yet.

I took pretty much every single drug we sold. I had never been a pill person, but I started doing those too—every day. With all the drugs I was taking and my lack of sleep, past trauma began to rear its ugly head. I started having drug-induced psychotic episodes. I often had flashbacks—but usually in my sleep. This was different. Much more than flashbacks, and it occurred in the middle of the day when I was wide awake. I could be having a conversation with somebody or driving in the car with Nick, and all of a sudden,

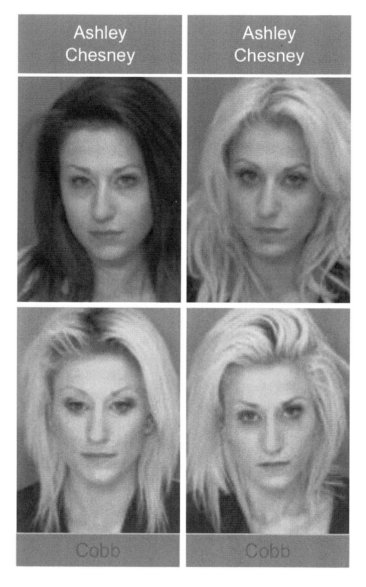

Nick was somebody else, and I was hallucinating and time traveling and reliving horrible experiences. Again and again, constantly, I went back to what happened in Missouri. I screamed and said things that didn't make any sense to the people with me. Nick was patient, perhaps because of his own trauma in the military. But it kept happening, and every time I finally came out of it, I would feel embarrassed, ashamed, and not want to discuss it.

Instead, I just kept getting high, masking the pain, going through the motions, body in overdrive, not eating, not sleeping. *Just keep pushing*, I told myself. *Hustle, keep grinding, get this money.* I ignored what my body was trying to tell me. I was really good at it by this point. After all, I'd had years of practice.

***

Nick and I got a new connection. Later on, he became one of my road dogs, but when we first encountered him, he was still in prison. I started talking to him on the phone, sending green dot cards (prepaid gift cards used as payment), and picking up work from him—this guy I had yet to meet in person. He was running an operation. And not even out on the streets.

Paranoia began to creep up on me. Nick and I were doing too much. We had too much supply and way too many people to meet. As my paranoia grew worse, I couldn't stay in the hotel rooms anymore, with all the guns and the driving back and forth—I felt like I was going crazy.

At this point, we were renting out my friend Allesandra's basement. She was a sweet girl who was smart, pretty, and lived alone, basically never leaving her house. She was an IV drug user like me, and we became fast friends. Her house was amazing, but it was never clean. It wasn't *dirty* like the trap houses I had been to, but she did have a lot of things and these things were everywhere. Not to mention the entire house was littered with orange needle caps.

When Allesandra said she was throwing a Fourth of July party, I was a little surprised.

"I do this every year," she said casually. "It's for my little cousin's birthday."

Not convinced, I looked at her like she had grown two heads. Allesandra was socially awkward, and I didn't realize she had friends outside the drug world.

Nick and I came home that night to a raging party. It was like a scene from a cheesy college movie. Her cousin was twenty-one, so there were hundreds of twenty-one-year-olds doing what they do best. People filled every room, and we could barely walk down the hallways. Beer pong, people in the pool, kids carrying lit tiki torches—*inside* the house. I found Allesandra just as happy as could be, which made me laugh. She looked like she didn't have a care in the world.

Meanwhile, Nick unloaded every single gun we had from the car and laid them across our bed. AKs, AR-15s, shotguns, pistols. He would get into moods like this sometimes, where he felt that certain checks and counts were necessary. I, however, popped some ecstasy pills *and* dropped some acid. Hey—it's a party, right?

We were getting ready to go join the land of the living upstairs when I realized I couldn't see.

My eyes wouldn't stop moving; they crossed on their own, and I couldn't walk. For the rest of the night, I sat with my eyes crossed. Nick shook his head at me and shrugged, laughing to himself. I'd probably been awake for two weeks, refusing to sleep.

"There's nothing I can do!" he told me when I shot him a pouty look from across the room.

You would think instances like this one would make me slow down or not do so many drugs. Nope. The thought did not even cross my mind.

As we listened to the wild party upstairs, Nick started to worry. He began pacing back and forth, his heart rate elevated. "There are too many people here. The cops are going to come."

His buddy tried to reassure him. "Chill out, man."

But Nick challenged, "Are you kidding me? Look at what we have in here. I can't just leave, but I need to lock our room somehow once the drop comes."

As I sat in a little ball, ashamed to look anybody in the eye, I listened to the predicament we were in. Nick was waiting for his pill connect; we couldn't leave until the guy got here.

"Ah, I wish he would hurry the fuck up," Nick murmured. Eventually he dismissed our friends. "You guys should go somewhere and we'll catch up with you later."

Then he and I waited.

The dude came and went, and Nick—also on acid—decided to spend way too much time counting out every single one of the pills. "I got everything he had," he said as I stared at the mounds and mounds of pills and tried to help him count while still cross eyed.

"How much money do we have left?" I asked.

"I used it all but like $100. Just chill. We will flip it so quick. My phone has been ringing off the hook. But first I have to count," he said again, getting agitated.

We were unprepared for what happened next.

Somebody said the police were here.

Nick and I locked our door leading into the garage and then stared at the entrance to our room: two French doors without a lock. We secured a combination lock on the outside, turned all the lights off, and sat on the floor shaking. I remember thinking I needed to move; we were sitting right where the doors parted, with piles of pills around us. All the cops had to do was open the door.

Nick's voice trembled as he whispered to me, "I am so sorry. Fuck. I just unloaded all the guns."

We literally had an arsenal lying across our bed. Swimming in pills, tripping on acid, we sat as still as we could and listened as the cops came downstairs. We could hear them talking to Alessandra. The party would have gotten busted either way, but lucky for them, they could kill two birds with one stone. Knowing what I know now, Nick and I were probably under investigation and didn't realize it at the time.

"Why is there a lock on this door?" they asked.

"Um, because my friends stay there. They rent it from me," Alessandra replied awkwardly, stumbling over her words.

"And do your friends have names? Where are they? They didn't want to attend your party?"

"Uh, Ashley and Nick, and they were here, but they left. So they probably locked it so nobody would go in and steal their stuff."

"Ashley and Nick, huh? Do they have a last name?"

One of the cops shined his flashlight through the crack between the French doors. I thought for sure they would see us—we were sitting *right* in front of them.

I remember having to pee so bad. I was shivering, and Nick begged me in a whisper-scream to please hold still. I had no control over my body, and I ended up peeing right there on the floor. Nick and I sat together and cried, knowing that if the cops got into this room, we were going to prison for a very long time.

"I don't have access to the lock," Alessandra protested. "I don't know the combination."

The cops pressed her and began getting frustrated. As they walked away, they said, "We'll be back with a warrant."

We had no way of knowing if they were truly gone. We'd turned off our phones to keep them from ringing or lighting up, and we were too scared to move. With an array of guns lying comfortably on the bed just five feet away, Nick and I sat on the pee-soaked floor violently shaking, holding each other for four hours.

The sun eventually came up. We packed everything incriminating into my car and then did what we always did. We drove and drove and drove.

CHAPTER 8

I did then what I knew how to do. Now that I know better, I do better.

—MAYA ANGELOU

Our connection finally got out of prison. His name was Paulo, and when he joined up with us, our drug enterprise became a whole new ball game.

I felt like I needed tinted windows just to drive in the car with him. He was tattooed from the top of his skull to his feet, and I looked like a blonde, strung-out Barbie. We were quite a sight. I took him to the mall one day, and little kids gathered around to ask for his autograph. I don't know if they thought he was a rapper or a professional athlete, but I can assure you he was neither of those things. And I hated all the attention. At this very mall, men often approached me and blatantly asked if I was a prostitute and how they could contact me. This used to make me so angry, but true to form, I would politely tell them no and try to ignore my inner urge to cuss them out. Maybe I just looked the part with my big platform shoes, feathers in my hair, minimal clothing. Or maybe I put out an energy to all perpetrators, abusers, and sex buyers that I *was* approachable in this way.

Around this time, Nick started buying mushrooms by the pound. I didn't understand why because nobody was buying them—but they were sure disappearing. What happened at Alessandra's Fourth of July party spooked us, but I think it spooked Nick more. He was eating mushrooms like it was his job instead of answering the phone and selling drugs, which was his real job.

Over time Paulo and I became close friends. I liked his girlfriend, and the four of us were pretty much inseparable. Paulo asked me one day, "What's up? Are you guys gonna get off this work?"

He didn't understand why we weren't making the same amount of money as before, when he was in prison. Nick and I weren't making quota anymore. We were barely selling anything because a lot of the time, Nick was so high he couldn't even talk. I began answering his phones that way: "Hi. Nick can't come to the phone right now. He's currently on mute, but can I help you?" It started as a joke. Until it wasn't funny anymore because it was true. He could not—would not?—talk. The mushrooms and the combination of other drugs made him stop speaking. It's like he just didn't care anymore.

I *did* care, so I began to take orders.

I embodied this invincible persona I had created. I channeled her. I had to if I wanted to survive. Paulo would rent new cars every week, and I would drive them. I was selling all of Nick's products *and* all of Paulo's, and pleased with myself, I began to feel like I was on top of the world.

One night after selling everything I had, I looked in the mirror and thought, *This must have been what Shelly felt like. This feeling right here. This is why people get caught up in the dope game.*

And just like it had with Shelly, the life I was living began to catch up with me. One day the cops pulled me over because (so they said) I'd been going five miles over the speed limit.

The officer who accused me of speeding ran my name and then came back to the car. I didn't get a ticket, and even though I had a bunch of dope with me, he didn't search the car. But he did give me a warning.

"You know your name comes up clean as far as your record goes, but it also says you're a known associate of Shelly Roberts and Andrew Long. You know them?" It was a trick question. Clearly I knew them, or my name wouldn't have come up on a police database saying so.

Shelly's brother had warned me, "The police are following you." And he was right.

I told the cop something about going in a different direction with my life, and he let me go.

Whenever the police showed up, or even if they got close, I would always volunteer to hold the dope or put guns in my purse—all to prove my loyalty. I was stupid. I'm not exactly sure who I needed to prove myself to, but I wanted people to know I was down. Especially Nick and Paulo. I knew that if either of them got arrested, they would be gone for a long time, but me? I had never been in trouble in my life. I assumed I would get a slap on the wrist, and the guys would immediately bond me out if anything happened. Because that's what friends do.

***

Paulo called me one night at 3:00 a.m. Nick and I were at Jessie's, hanging out in our bedroom, maybe watching *Breaking Bad* or searching blackhead videos on YouTube. Our usual 3:00 a.m. activities.

"Yo, what are you guys doing?" Paulo asked happily. "Come over. I have a room."

"What are *you* doing?" I asked, laughing at his energetic tone.

"I just got the best coke ever."

"Coke?"

We laughed and bantered back and forth. Nick and I waited for the sun to come up and then drove over to Motel 6 to meet Paulo. He was right—the coke was good. I don't think I had done cocaine since high school. Maybe once or twice while working at the strip club. These days, my typical poisons were meth and room-temperature Jack Daniel's.

We hung out that day. I don't remember it being different from any other day we were with Paulo. People came and went, picked up sacks of dope or pills, and eventually it was time to leave.

We stepped one foot out of the room—and spotted the police knocking on the motel's doors. All three of us practically sprinted to my car. I hopped in the driver's seat amidst Paulo freaking me out. He didn't help at all as he yelled, "You need to go! You need to go now!"

"I'm trying!" I replied and nearly fumbled the key as I inserted it into the ignition, hands trembling.

Cop cars and blacked-out SUVs were parked everywhere. Though we made it out of the motel parking lot and onto the highway, I saw one of the SUVs pull out behind us. They weren't exactly on our tail, but I knew what we had in the car and I did not want to be followed.

I have never driven so fast in my life. I took off-ramps and on-ramps, side streets and backroads, just to get back on the interstate. Nick and Paulo both screamed directions at me, talking about the steady tail behind us. I drove like a maniac and somehow managed to lose the cops.

I will never forget the way I felt that night. My clenched feet, my heart beating out of my chest, every nerve in me vibrating as I drove. The feeling of elation when I realized we'd lost them, that we were safe. But the comedown was real—I think for the first time in weeks, I actually slept.

***

August 10, 2012.

The days, weeks, and months blend together for me in an ombre of memories. I didn't sleep much, so there was no reset. No easy way to differentiate one day from the next. I can't tell you what we did that morning, but I know we went to Brad's in the afternoon.

Brad lived in a known drug house. He rented the bottom floor from an elderly couple, and anyone and everyone I knew in the drug scene had partied there at some point along their journey. When Nick and I showed up, a bunch of our "friends" were already there, and people were acting weird as per usual.

Brad offered to sell Nick a dirty pistol with the serial number scratched off, and Nick bought the .380 like a dumbass. We didn't bring all our drugs inside because you never knew what might happen at that house. I didn't fully trust Brad or anyone there. Drama happened too often around these folks.

Suddenly somebody came in and said, "The cops are circling the cul-de-sac."

I ran outside to get the rest of our stash as panic quickly took over the room.

Reggie, a friend of ours, kept trying to tell Nick what to do. "Take your backpack full of work, take the guns, and walk with me out the back. We can walk over to the Big Lots parking lot, and Ash can pick us up there. Have her ride clean. That way if the cops pull her over, they got nothing."

It seemed logical, but I remember a distinct feeling of mistrust. Anxious energy permeated the room like everybody else knew something Nick and I did not.

Nick was headstrong and, as I mentioned, hadn't been in his right mind the last few months. He argued with Reggie. "No, fuck that. I'm not leaving her, and I'm not staying here—let's go." He gestured for me to walk out.

I don't believe Nick thought he was invincible. Not now. After all, we had been given too many chances. Too many close calls. Yet we still lived as recklessly as ever. I think he assumed that if we got pulled over, he would take the rap and I wouldn't go to jail. Not only was I naive when it came to police interactions, but I was also deep in my addiction. Nick didn't know this, but I had drugs stashed everywhere. In my purse, my bra. It was my "just-in-case stash" if Nick and I ever got separated.

We climbed in the car and started to drive away. I remember how hot it was that day. My legs stuck to the seat, and I thought, *I'm so glad Nick's not wearing his vest.* He used to wear that stupid bulletproof vest every day.

As I drove onto the main road, they got us.

Two cops immediately pulled into the lanes next to us, one eagerly trying to get behind us. I weaved in and out of traffic to prevent them from pulling us over, and we drove a total of three minutes before they boxed us in and escorted us onto the shoulder.

I had a gun and my personal stash of pills in my purse, as well as the assortment of drugs in my bra. Nick had two firearms on him, including the dirty one he had just purchased from Brad, and a laptop bag full to the brim of drugs lying out on my backseat.

As the police ran our licenses, Nick's phones started ringing off the hook. He kept picking them up and slamming them down on the dashboard in a strange attempt to get them to stop making noise, instead of just turning them off. The officer eyed us suspiciously.

They arrested Nick first, as soon as they ran his name. He was on felony probation and in possession of firearms. He sat in handcuffs as they searched my car. I had no record whatsoever, not even a parking ticket, but they knew who we were and they were going to pin something on me. When they searched my purse, their eyes widened and they pulled out the police edition Glock 19. I knew damn well I would never use that gun but kept it on me anyway. They unscrewed my little metal pill case keychain containing an array of pills and went through my makeup bag. Popped open a blue plastic case, and Roxys came tumbling out. They put me in handcuffs and told me to wait for a female officer.

Nick was angry. They put us in separate cars, and he kept mouthing things to me through the window. I couldn't understand what he was saying. Finally, an officer stepped in front of the window and blocked my view of him.

What felt like hours later, a female officer arrived on the scene. She hopped in the front seat of the vehicle, read me my Miranda rights, and started asking me questions about pictures on my phone. I used to love Tumblr, that photo blogging website. I would spend hours geeking out on that website, saving photos I liked. (This was before Instagram was cool, okay?) Anyway, I had saved tons of photographs of guns bedazzled in diamonds, Hello Kitty shotguns, and model-like girls blowing out colored smoke and snorting lines. These were not real pictures, but given what the police knew about us, they looked incriminating. The officer wanted to know where the *rest* of our guns were, and I realized somebody had been talking to them. One of our "friends."

Nick and I discovered later that we had been under investigation for some time. They'd been following us for months. We did a lot of driving, a lot of hotel rooms, a whole lot of movement to prevent *this exact thing* from happening, and honestly, I'm in awe that they were still able to track us. But they did. Apparently, trapping out of motel rooms made their job easier than we suspected, since the people we sold drugs to would turn around and sell to undercovers in the parking lot. This traffic stop was premeditated.

The officer would not let up about the phone photos. She kept going back to this one picture of about ten guns lying out, all fancy and different colors, with jewels covering them.

I started laughing at her. "Those are not real pictures. I saved them off Tumblr. Do you know what Tumblr is?"

She did not appreciate this response. Maybe she thought I was lying, or maybe she was mad at herself for not putting two and two together that the guns we had were *not* dipped in gold and sparkly.

"If you're not going to talk," she said coldly, "you're going to jail." She climbed out of the car and slammed the door.

I burst into tears, shaking, and didn't know how to get myself out of this situation. I also didn't realize at the time that I had a choice in all of this. I didn't need to talk to the police at all. That's what I should have done—just remained silent.

The officer took me out of the car and searched me. I was wearing a skin-tight black dress with a corset-like bra underneath. She commented on my attire and then made me take the bra off on the side of the road. That's when the meth and coke fell out. I sat on the curb, defeated, kicking myself for *needing* to have drugs on me at all times. We were already getting charged with sixteen counts of narcotics from what was in the laptop bag—I didn't need to rack up any more charges based on my personal drug habit.

We were on our way to jail.

***

Intake in the Cobb County Jail is freezing. Bare white brick walls surround you and chill you to the bone.

All I wanted was a sweatshirt and to lie down and sleep. They strip-searched me again when we got to the jail, making me take out my hair extensions, and I had already cried my fake eyelashes off. I was a mess. Every time I tried to make myself into a little ball on the chair to keep warm, an officer would yell, "Feet on the floor."

Waiting for booking, the girls sat in chairs on the left, and the guys sat in chairs on the right, with an aisle in between. There were holding cells all around, with inmates who were further along in the dreaded process and waiting to go back to their dorms. The guys yelled things through the slots in the doors, catcalling and carrying on.

The officers allowed us to make phone calls in this room. As I walked up to make mine, feeling pitiful, a guy yelled, "Don't cry, baby," and I wanted to punch him in the throat.

Who do I call? I thought suddenly. I couldn't call my family—I wasn't ready for that. Nick told me to call Jessie; hers was the one number I had memorized and only because it was also her garage door code. I was so messed up all the time that I couldn't retain too much information: a phone number *and* a code?

I called her and explained what was happening as if she didn't already know. News travels fast in the drug world. I wanted to warn her because all our stuff was at her house, and I wanted to make sure she and her family were safe. I didn't know the bond-out process, but I pleaded with her to somehow get me out of there.

***

The events leading up to that day make more sense now.

According to my discovery packet, they'd been watching us for three months. That meant Alessandra's Fourth of July party, the few times the cops pulled me over for a taillight or for speeding and then let me go, the blacked-out SUVs on the highway, the chase from Motel 6, even Paulo's release from prison—I think it was all a setup. Including Paulo. It seems likely that he was a confidential informant, and I believe he was doing fed time and they used him for this operation. I don't know why the Georgia Bureau of Investigation (better known as the GBI) had nothing better to do but to follow Nick and me around for three months, but apparently, it was worth something to them. I was not anyone special, but I think they learned who we were connected to and thought they could take us all down.

I spent a few weeks in jail and slowly realized I was wrong thinking all the "homies" would bail me out if I ever got popped. In their defense, I think my mother accidentally flagged me. She had no prior experience with the judicial system, and when she found out where I was, she began calling bail bonds and explaining that she was in California and I had no family in Georgia, so I immediately became a flight risk. That meant no bond. Not initially, anyway. Nick was on his way to prison with a probation violation. But not right away. Georgia is notorious for dragging out court dates, and Cobb County is no exception. We did not go to court for almost eight months.

I was finally able to make bond by agreeing to participate in "pre-trial," a program where you're put on probation while awaiting sentencing. I had to check in with an officer and test clean while I waited for my trial. I said and signed whatever they wanted me to at that point—I just wanted out of jail and back on the streets.

They finally released me.

***

Without Nick, all the money, and the drugs, I went back to dancing. I had tried my hand at being a dope girl. And failed. I was done selling drugs.

I still did dope here and there, trying to do better but failing miserably. Jessie allowed me to stay at her house, but that in itself felt suffocating. I knew she didn't really want me there. I think there was some unspoken resentment that I was free and Nick, her friend of fifteen years, was locked up. She probably also dealt with underlying worries about her address, not to mention her family and protection, somehow being tied to us in the midst of an investigation. I'm sure she blamed me for causing Nick's downfall. I was thankful for a place to stay, but I tried not to be there very often.

Everybody held me at a distance. I was "hot," meaning we had just gotten busted, and I'm sure there were rumors as to who was working with the cops and all that nonsense. Everyone who does drugs can get a bit paranoid. And they have every right to be, considering what happened to me.

Besides Jessie, whose relationship with me had obviously changed, I had two girlfriends. Alessandra and Madison. Have you ever seen the show *Criminal Minds*? Madison was a much prettier version of the blonde, quirky agent with the glasses, who was always on the computer. Yup, that was Madi. She did dope, but she had every new contraption, every cool gadget; she knew the best hotels to go to in the city, the best places to get food. We were always doing something fun or organizing something. She would put Mio flavored water in the meth bong, take trips to the container store, and spin our own milkshakes at QuickTrip. She was a ball of light and super resourceful. If I ever found myself in another crisis, I hoped it would be with Madison. She seemed to always know what to do.

I got a job at the Pink Pony in Atlanta. I worked the day shift and made really good money. It's a higher-end strip club frequented by business executives and Falcon football players.

One night Madison picked me up. She was in the process of moving out of her apartment, and she mentioned to me, "I'm not really supposed to bring friends over because of my roommate."

Curious, I looked over at her.

"Do you know Chase?" she asked.

"I've heard his name," I replied. He had a reputation as one of the bigger dope dealers at the time. "But I have never met him."

She grinned. "Ah, he'll get over it—I'll just tell him I'm bringing home a stripper."

Chase was tall, tan, well built, and extremely well dressed. Not at all what I was expecting.

"You could have prepared me a little bit more for *that*," I jokingly whispered to Madison. We did introductions, and I could see him silently eyeing Madison in a way that said, "You know better than to bring people here." But there was also another energy in the room: our mutual attraction.

He was reserved at first. On edge. He was packing boxes and explaining how he'd just bought a townhouse. Maybe he was stressed from moving, yet stress comes with the territory. Dealing drugs brings challenges and requires constant hypervigilance. Unless you want to get caught.

Madi and I smoked a bowl, and he didn't touch it. I could see him trying to get a read on me, perhaps for his own safety or because he was simply curious. Eventually he warmed up. He flirted and smiled, showing perfectly white teeth. I already knew I wanted him, and I was gonna get him.

"You should come to visit me at work," I said coyly before we left.

"Where's work?" he replied.

"Pony," I said.

"Oh, I'll be there," he said and made a comment about his frequent visits to strip clubs. He and Madi laughed. I didn't get the joke.

***

As I heard more of his story, I learned that Chase had dated a girl named Alli on and off for the last seven years. One look at Chase, and it was no secret why the girls came around, but add what he did for a living to the mix and you had a *lot* of girls flocking. Alli was a bartender at Cheetah, one of the nicest strip clubs in Atlanta. Needless to say, their relationship had a lot of ups and downs. I happened to show up when they were down.

Everything happened so quickly with Chase. He came to my work one night, I left with him, and he asked me to live with him the next day. Happily ever after, right? Except a seven-year relationship doesn't usually just disappear, especially when you move your new twenty-one-year-old girlfriend into your house. Alli sometimes showed up, causing a scene. This happened periodically, but Chase was loyal to me. At least, he was in the beginning.

The ten-year gap between us also proved to be challenging. It wasn't so much the ten years, but it was the ten years with me being twenty-one. Things I thought were funny, he didn't. Things I wanted to experience, he already had. This proved to be a slight disconnect to what otherwise was a relationship with a ton of chemistry.

He was so careful. So safe. I had been around lots of people who sold drugs, but nobody operated like he did. Chase never did business at our house. He rarely went out driving past 10:00 p.m. He wouldn't take me to re-up on his supply or drop anything off, which separated me from ever being associated with his business. This was very unlike the situation with Nick, where I became immersed in what he was doing. Chase made an effort to be home every night, or we would get hotel rooms—usually the best of the best. He was fancy; he took self-care to a new level, and I liked to joke with him about it, when I secretly found it quite appealing.

I fell quickly and hard for Chase. My usual approach when I liked a guy. I was on pre-trial for my prior charges, although you couldn't tell by the way I was living. I was deep in my addiction and masked it well. I was at the point that if I couldn't get high the way *I* wanted to, then I didn't want to use meth at all. Chase, Madison, and the majority of my "friends" were against using a needle. There's like this caliber of meth users. A hierarchy tier. This was funny to me because Chase could put a steroid needle in his butt cheek, chew Xanax bars like candy, and smoke meth out of a pipe, but I was considered the lowest of the low because I stuck a needle in my arm.

This new group of friends also used GHB. It's a liquid, and a little goes a long way. Take more than a bottle cap, and you're gone. It is the date rape drug that depresses your central nervous system, but if you take it in smaller doses, you don't pass out and it has similar euphoric effects as ecstasy. Because I wasn't able to do meth how I wanted (oh no! A needle!), I began bringing GHB with me to work and taking shots before my shift. Just to detach, to leave, to be able to take my clothes off for money.

The story of my life.

CHAPTER 9

The game ends when you have the freedom to truly be yourself.

—KH

I began to see red flags with Chase.

Maybe because I was sneaking around trying to get high, and he was sneaking around trying to see Alli. But his relationship with her escalated, and it often felt like he was dating us both. When he wasn't with me, he was with her. It was a vicious cycle that he would complete when he returned home to tell me how much he loved me and that we should get married. I was crazy and believed him. He took me to meet his family; we spent Thanksgiving and Christmas with them, and I genuinely thought we were in love. He'd take me to hotel rooms costing $1,000 a night and then bam—we'd fight. Things always got physical and he would leave. We were either hot or ice cold.

"The reason I go with Alli is because *you* shoot dope," he'd say.

A justification for cheating on me. He was gaslighting me— it was *my* fault he continually cheated. He placed the blame in my court, and I would respond by doing exactly what he said: shooting dope. The control tactics and roller-coaster highs and lows blinded me. I thought it was normal, because I didn't realize what a healthy relationship looked like, and I couldn't see through the haze of meth smoke.

He put cameras up in every room of our house. The only exception was the bathroom, and I would lock myself in there for hours as I got ready for work. Just to have peace of mind without being watched. When he left, he turned his phones off. *He's with Alli,* I assumed. But then friends would tell me that Chase was at their house watching me on the cameras. If he wanted to know what I was doing so badly, why not just come home?

The door to our house had an electronic lock. He would ghost me, turn off his phones, and change my personal code to the door. When that happened, I didn't care who he was with. I was just angry. All my things were locked inside a place someone else controlled.

When you're on meth, time slips from you. I don't know where it goes, but it simply vanishes. It takes hours to do anything and even longer to do anything productive. My attempts at getting a dose in my arm would turn into these long, drawn-out escapades, and sometimes I forgot to turn my phone off silent, caught up in the race against time. If Chase called and I didn't answer, he would just go with somebody else. It felt like punishment. I had a small window in which to please him and no margin for error. If I failed, it was over.

I felt like I couldn't tell him the truth. I just wanted to get high, much like he did but in a different way. When I couldn't get back into our house, I would usually go to Alessandra's. She would help me get high, and then I would hang out there or go shopping. It's possible I adopted a shopping addiction at some point during this time. A guilty pleasure that was probably the least threatening of all the addictions I held. I spent all the money I earned at work on clothes as I shopped by myself. I often felt ashamed about it and couldn't tell Chase where I was. So some of the time while he thought I was being sneaky, I really was just at the mall. It was what I liked to do by myself after getting high. I don't know why I kept it a secret.

***

I was still doing drugs as my pre-trial testing day approached. Chase bought me some contraption that would allow me to use fake urine for the test. I wore a baggy sweatshirt to hide what I'd strapped to my body.

He dropped me off at the courthouse. As ordered, I entered the bathroom and, with the officer's eyes politely averted, was able to "pee" into the toilet. The thing worked! But as I tried to pull up my pants, the cord draped like a tail out the end of my sweatshirt. Busted. I was sanctioned to thirty days in jail.

Another time they told me to report, I said, "Fuck it. I'm gonna run." I was at Madison's house, and I wanted to use so bad. I couldn't bear to wait a whole twenty-four hours. So I gave in and spent the next fourteen hours looking at hospitals I could check myself into for the night to avoid my pre-trial court date with a reasonable excuse. I ended up checking myself into Peachford Hospital's detox/mental health program just to bypass the courts, all for the sake of a fix.

Chase came to visit me there. He rarely answered the phone when I called from the hospital, but he showed up one day for visitation. Guests were required to check their phones at reception, and clearly embarrassed, he handed over three cell phones.

He walked up to me, and even before he got to me, I could see the long black hair sticking to his orange polo shirt. It sounds like the crazy girlfriend thing to say. "I found a hair on your shirt!" But seriously, I can't make this stuff up. It was that obvious. He just didn't care.

"You didn't even bother to look down at your shirt before you walked in?" I asked coldly, knowing Alli was probably waiting for him in the parking lot.

He laughed. That's how our relationship went with him. The jokes, the brush-offs, the complete disregard for the fact that he was playing with two people's hearts. I do not doubt that this experience was painful for Alli as well. Whether she suspected this or not, I knew *exactly* how she felt.

But no matter what happened between us, Chase and I would make up and the pattern would start again. Sprawled out on the bed, Chase would say sweetly, "Please don't go to work tonight. Stay here with me."

The words I longed to hear, as I constantly craved his attention and the knowledge that *I* was worth choosing. This emotionally abusive merry-go-round played a repetitive tune: *Choose me, choose me, please choose me.* I never realized that I shouldn't be with somebody who viewed me just as an option. I began to believe that I was his second priority, so when he treated me like his first, I felt like I'd won and I didn't want to give up my spot.

Knowing I needed to go to work, I would reply, "I can't skip work. I have to make money."

To which he'd say, "I got you, girl." Every damn time. This cycle repeated, and we'd spend three days together at home or in a hotel, with everything perfect. Until he would have to go pick up or run an errand. Then suddenly I could no longer reach him.

CHAPTER 9

Sleep together, go pick up, ghost me, repeat.

Unavailable, emotionally and physically. And there I was, without money, without options, without provisions because he didn't let me go to work. Was this what he meant by "I got you, girl"? Yeah, he got me all right. It was so painful that my heart ached. Unknowingly, I was addicted to emotional chaos that I mistook for love. At this point, I was numb to my real emotions and used to feeling nothing. So if I was able to feel anything resembling pain, it must have been agonizing.

One day I told him I was going to get an apartment in Virginia Highland, but the minute I started packing my things, he convinced me to stay. I was stuck—I wanted him more than I wanted to take care of myself. I kept missing opportunities to make money because he would pull these cards on the weekend, which were my most high-paying days at the club, and then Monday I would be left to rot without anything. I didn't have enough to put down a security deposit on an apartment, let alone actually rent one.

I began to get tired. Tired of coming home after work to see his truck in the driveway, but I couldn't get inside the house. Tired of thinking other girls were in *my* house, with all my belongings. Tired of finding my things missing when I finally did get inside. Tired of feeling broke for the sake of somebody else who, I finally started to realize, didn't truly love me.

I moved all my stuff to Alessandra's.

✳✳✳

Living with Alessandra was like getting together with a best friend and catching up with one another after an extended absence. We had no other agenda than meth, so our "catch-ups" lasted two weeks. Everything I owned just sat in her living room. I had no need for a bed because I never slept.

My court date for the charges I'd racked up with Nick was right around the corner. I hated my lawyer and didn't understand the severity of anything going on around me. My mom called one day and tried to walk me through some of the possible outcomes.

But I just snapped at her. "I don't know and I don't care what happens to me."

I stayed awake for fourteen days leading up to my court date. Chase could not be found the morning of, and I felt so alone and helpless.

I also felt entitled. The possibility that I could end up going to prison never even crossed my mind. I didn't think I would even go to jail.

And I was right. Despite my bad attitude, I left the courtroom that day with a slap on the wrist. Ten years first offender's probation. Since I'd never been in trouble before, the charges would be expunged from my record *if* I completed my probation without getting in trouble again. I left the courtroom that day and stuck a needle in my arm in celebration.

***

I constantly felt like I was walking around with a big balloon full of air inside me. Project outward. Look good. Be strong. Be hard. When in actuality I was scared and viewed everything and everyone through a lens of possible threat.

Alessandra, being my most loyal friend, never judged me or commented on any decision I made, even if it was a poor one. She was one of the few people who talked to me about God.

Even though I didn't believe, I knew she did, and I felt I could deflate my balloon around her. I didn't have to pretend when I was with her. She provided a sort of assurance within me that allowed me to breathe. I could put down the façade of my superficial, high-stress state and just be me without judgment. Maybe I needed somebody like her, whom I trusted with my balloon, to look at my situation closely and speak into it. Maybe I needed somebody to stand up and say something about the way I was behaving.

Finally, after hearing me cry over Chase, money, and all my struggles for the hundredth time, she reacted gently. I will never forget the way she looked at me. I was standing right outside her bathroom, and she glanced at me through the doorway. She paused, seemed to consider her words, and said, "Ashley, why don't you go home to California?"

It was unlike Alessandra to say something that challenged me, and yet the way she said it was kind and completely caught me off guard. I had never considered California to be an option. Why *was* I still struggling out here in Georgia? Very little good had come out of my decision to stay here.

I think God, in His sweetness and even in my unbelief, was trying to warn me. This quiet conversation with Alessandra was one of two warnings I received.

Living the sheltered—and dare I say *privileged*—life that I did growing up, I always wondered what the "other side" was like. One day I finally got to experience the other side and got stuck there. It just grabbed me, and I felt like I couldn't escape. I began to feel guilty for giving up the beautiful life I had, and to deal with both sides of this duality, I kept using. Running from the guilt I had caused myself and, even more, my family.

The second divine warning I received came one night when Madison asked me to party with her. She was going to a friend's house out in Cumming, Georgia. It's funny because that's where Emma lived, my friend who picked me up from Missouri. Cumming was my first Georgia experience, and I felt like I'd come full circle.

At the end of the forty-mile drive, I pulled up to a nice house. I was wearing cork wedges, a long hippie sweater with fringe (I loved that dang sweater), and jeans. I didn't expect anything unusual to happen that night. I just thought we would party, hang out, talk. It was good to see Madison again, and I met her friend Jaden.

I always had dope so we passed the pipe around. Maybe we did lines; who knows? I talked about Chase and let them know what was going on. Both Jaden and Madison had known Chase for years. They saw my pain but also knew Alli was a constant crutch in his life. She wasn't going anywhere. They didn't try to convince me of anything, but they listened intently and told me the facts. In a sense, I was new to this world and to these people, and I didn't have the history they did. So I also did my best to listen, trying to soak it all in while my heart sat in my chest lying to me.

In the midst of all of this, Jaden pulled out some DMT.

DMT is a hallucinogenic drug that produces effects similar (but less intense, in my opinion) to LSD or mushrooms. This is one way Healthline.com describes it:

> Some experts believe the pineal gland produces it in the brain and releases it when we dream. Others believe it's released during birth and death. Some go

further to say this release of DMT at death may be
responsible for those mystical near-death experiences
you sometimes hear about.[1]

You know the feeling you get when you are 100 percent self-
assured? That moment when nobody could change your mind, and
you are fully committed to walking forward with your decision?
Well, as a trauma survivor, I *rarely* got that feeling. I struggled
with decision-making for as long as I could remember, and much
of the time, especially during times of high stress, I went back and
forth between two choices until my brain was exhausted and I
never fully arrived at a conclusion. But that night with Jaden and
Madison, that self-assured feeling came and, drug induced or not,
it was real. I knew with certainty what I needed to do.

I needed to leave Chase.

It was as clear as day, as if the fog that kept me stuck lifted from
my brain. I felt knowingness down to my bones. This was the right
choice. There was absolutely no reason for me to stay with somebody who could not commit to me, who sold drugs and constantly
kept me in a state of dependence on him. What on earth had I been
doing? My behavior up until this point was almost comical.

That was another time God nudged me. He impressed the
truth upon my heart, guiding me in the right direction. Isn't that
like God? There I was living a life full of sin, high on drugs, and
He still pursued me. He attempted to nudge my spirit, to give me
the self-assurance to go the better way. That night I came up with
a whole plan about what I would do with my belongings, where I
would live, what I would do for work, everything.

---

[1] "Everything You Need to Know About DMT, the 'Spirit Molecule,'" Healthline, accessed Nov. 27, 2021,
https://www.healthline.com/health/what-is-dmt.

Yet as the drugs faded, and my phone started ringing and displaying Chase's name, I didn't leave. I once again bypassed myself.

**

I changed clubs again.

I was tired of working the day shift, tired of the fake "gentleman's club" act where I pretended we *weren't* at a strip club. I was tired of old white men and a lack of rap music. I was wild and I was running.

One day when I voiced my opinion in the locker room, one of the other girls told me, "You should go work at Follies. They play *real* strip club music, and rappers come in there all the time. You would be one of the only white girls. I used to make a lot of money doing that."

She sold me at "a lot of money," so I switched.

Walking into the club that first night, I didn't know if I would be able to dance or if they would even take me on. It was a small club. Nothing special.

I stepped into the owner's office and introduced myself. "Hi. I'm Ryann," I said and handed him the permit that allowed me to work at all the clubs in the Atlanta area.

"So let me get this straight," he said, looking surprised. "You have a valid permit *and* you want to work *here*?"

I'm guessing I was a rarity for this club, even more so because of the color of my skin. The county requires dancers to have an entertainment license that costs around $350.00. Many times clubs will allow girls to work without permits until they can afford one, but then the girls never go obtain it. Police sometimes do sweeps through the clubs checking for permits, drugs, and guns and arresting those who don't meet the requirements.

Needless to say, I got the job. But I honestly don't know what was going on in my head at the time. Changing from Pony to Follies was not a good career choice. I was a skeleton with long blonde extensions. I did meth so I was automatically awkward, weird, and suspicious. And probably the biggest bust of them all is I could not dance like these other girls even when I tried—I was simply skin and bones. I made some money, but nothing like what I was used to. Chase came to visit me from time to time, probably because he wanted to check up on me, but it helped. He would start throwing money at me, and as if it were a competition, other guys would start too.

The club was ghetto and the cops frequently raided it. Sometimes there were shootings right outside, which caused the club to go on lockdown. We weren't allowed to leave until the area was clear, which meant we girls had to sleep on pool tables or sit around waiting to drive home. The club closed at 4:00 a.m., and some nights I wouldn't get home until 7:00 in the morning. Two nights in a row, some of the other girls raided my locker. The first night they took my makeup bag and the second night a bag of outfits. Power move. I wasn't making enough money to tolerate stuff like that—I didn't care that Gucci Mane and Drake visited the club or that Future rapped about it. I was out of place and it showed.

We were required to breathalyze before leaving the club each night. Security guards walked us to our cars, and we were not allowed to leave with customers. However, I often saw girls who were too drunk to drive abandon their cars in the club parking lot and run across Buford Highway to the QuikTrip and jump into a car with a customer.

Strip clubs are not innocent. VIP rooms and what happens after hours are all rooted in exploitation, prostitution, and even trafficking.

***

One night I blew above the limit. Shit. I couldn't drive, so I called Chase to pick me up. I figured he would be at home because he was never out this late, but he was always up. It was 3:00 in the morning. Tipsy and giggly, I assumed I would have to flirt to convince him to come get me, but he answered on the first ring. I could tell he was in his truck; the window was down.

"Please come get me," I said. "I can't drive."

"Aw, Ash, are you drunk? Okay, I'll be right there," he said in the sweet, sing-song tone he used whenever he was in a good mood.

The fact that he was out and about should have been a red flag to me because it was so out of character for him and likely meant one of two things: He went to pick up, or he went to deliver. Neither of those things should happen at 3:00 a.m., so whatever it was, it must have been important.

When he arrived, I hopped into his truck, threw my bag in the back, and smiled at him.

"I have a suite at the Marriott," he said, explaining that people were coming to meet him. His private party had apparently already started; he was amped up as if it weren't the middle of the night.

Everything seemed off to me. The people coming to meet him were not his usual clientele. They were what we referred to as "J'd out" junkies and sack chasers.

That month I had finally learned how to hit myself. I didn't have to drive around the state of Georgia in secret trying to get somebody to shoot me up anymore. This was a blessing and a curse. Of course, Chase didn't know. As he served some randoms in our hotel room, I made up a dose in the bathroom.

Knocking on the door, he announced, "I want to drop off some work in Cobb County."

The place was notorious for cops, and it was also where I got arrested.

"No, thanks," I said, focused on the task at hand. His mood was concerning me a little, plus I also wanted to stay in the room by myself. Then I could get high.

Maybe he caught on to that last part—he hated that part of me.

"You know what?" he fumed. "Fuck it, you're coming with me. You're not gonna stay in *my* room." Taking ownership for something he paid for, which happened a lot with us. He'd invite me to partake in his lifestyle as his significant other, his girlfriend. He would share the luxuries with me when it was convenient for him, buying me things, taking me shopping—and then take those things away the minute we started fighting. I would suddenly lose all privileges and be treated as if I were some peasant mooching off of him.

As punishment for arguing with him, I was now forced to ride with him from Atlanta to Marietta at close to 4:00 a.m. He switched cars, moving some things from his truck to his brand-new Infiniti G35. As we drove, he spoke to someone on the phone, and I listened in, trying to figure out who we were meeting. Who on earth could be this important?

We pulled up to a janky motel. Turned out that *nobody* was this important. I think it might have been the same gross motel where the cops told me to get as far away from Ron as I could. My time in Georgia had come full circle again, and here I sat dangerously vulnerable in a motel parking lot.

I was still salty from our argument, holding my silence like a badge of honor in the passenger's seat. He made some phone calls announcing our arrival. Scott, one of Chase's best friends, was parked a few spaces down. Also waiting.

An eerie silence draped over us as we waited for the two girls he'd planned to meet for this "special occasion." As they made their way downstairs, the silence splintered into jerky movements as Chase gathered his things and prepped to go greet the girls.

I reached over, opened my passenger side door, and looked up as cop lights flooded the parking lot.

CHAPTER 10

Growth and comfort do not coexist.

—GINNI ROMETTY

Chase and I stared at each other.

He began chewing up the Xanax bars he had in his pocket, throwing them on the ground, stepping on them. I had a loaded rig in my bag, my own personal stash of dope, and a bunch of random Adderall pills some junkie had given to me as collateral when he couldn't pay me for the meth I'd brought him. The only thing I could do was slide the rig inside the sleeve of my sweatshirt.

It all happened so fast, so fluidly.

I had been running for a long time, had lived in a state of fear for years, and my body just didn't have the stamina to compete with this sudden new stress. My brain, wired for acute stress responses, ran out of juice.

The police talked to Chase, who was on probation. Another cop asked one of the girls if they could go up and search her room. I have no idea why she said yes. She and her friend were now going to jail.

A German Shepherd drug dog began sniffing around the cars. It immediately hit on our car, and I thought darkly, *Well, obviously!* Not impressed as I stared at the large Tupperware container of meth lying openly on the backseat.

Chase's friend Scott was hiding on the ground underneath his truck. The dog hit on Scott's truck as well—but then kept going, leaving him safe underneath the vehicle. *Stupid dog.* What I would have given to be Scott that night.

The police began casually questioning me as I sat in Chase's car with the door open, my legs sprawled over the seat.

"What were you guys doing?"

"I don't know," I replied. "I just got off from work—he picked me up."

"Where do you work?"

This conversation with two male officers quickly turned sour. They assumed I was a prostitute; I could tell when I said the club's name. They began questioning how I was dressed, asking how I knew Chase, etc. They thought I was "working," when I was just with my boyfriend and happened to be wearing shorts in the middle of the night. I felt dirty, unseen, and outnumbered. They never called a female officer to the scene.

Chase must have picked up *just* before coming to grab me at the club. Another thing he had never done—put me in a car with a bunch of dope. He was always super considerate of that kind of thing. But not tonight.

They searched my purse, which led to me sitting in handcuffs on the curb. Out of the cops' eyesight, I was able to throw the loaded rig from the sleeve of my sweatshirt into the bushes. I knew the pills and dope in my purse guaranteed me a ride back

CHAPTER 10

to jail. In addition to the half-pound of meth sitting in Chase's backseat. We all were going down.

They loaded me into one of the cars. I looked over at Chase and the two girls sitting there in handcuffs, and when he caught my eye, he mouthed to me, "Get yourself out of this."

The patty wagon door slammed. Keeping me separate from everyone else, the male officers began to ask me a lot of questions, and I, out of desperation, began to plead with them.

"Please help me get into a program." I told them the truth: "I *just* got put on probation a month ago." It had been twelve whole days since my sentencing hearing. Twelve days into my ten-year probation sentence that was going to clear my record if I complied. I didn't even make it one month. It was March 17, my mom's birthday. That thought played like a loop over and over in my head: "Happy birthday, Mom."

I don't remember much of the conversation as I sat in the back of the police car, but at one point, I cried—begged for a chance. Begged for help. When they didn't soften to the fact that I had a drug problem, I tried another avenue. The officer to my right seemed the easiest to break. He was about my dad's age, and I asked him, "Do you have daughters?"

I didn't have the words for human trafficking yet, but I began telling him things I had never said out loud before. I told him about Missouri and how I got to Georgia in the first place. I told him I worked in the clubs to survive. I remember him looking at me and looking back at his partner. I could feel him on the fence of mercy. He offered me a deal.

I took it.

He even let me drive Chase's car out of there. I went straight to Alessandra's house and stuck a needle in my arm. What in the literal heck was wrong with me? I was jittery; my body was in shock, and I could not stop shaking. I couldn't make sense of what happened.

I had Chase's credit card in my back pocket. He'd left it with me, intending that I pay the bills and handle responsibilities for him. Well, I went to our hotel where a hundred green Xanax bars sat in a safe. I popped a couple, a drug I didn't even like, and then went to the mall. I let the pills calm my system, and the constant intensity I was so used to feeling began to fade to the background. Adrenaline began to dull. And I bought new jeans.

I was out of my mind. Alli began calling me. Then Chase's parents started calling. Both parties trying to figure out what was going on. I finally went home when I realized Chase had given Alli the codes to the safes. Because he was wiped out, she took all the drugs, the money, his electronics—anything that might incriminate him. At that moment, I realized he trusted her more than he trusted me. I had no room to argue as brand-new $200 jeans hung on my hips, but I felt entitled to the things he'd entrusted to her. To me, *I* was the one living there. It was *my* home. *I* should not be the one out of dope and out of money. This felt like a slap in the face.

Resentment built slowly in my chest. "Chase put me in a position to ride with him that night," I said to myself. Defensiveness dripped from my tongue. I used whatever I could not to feel. To avoid the guilt of the arrests, my behaviors, and the part I played. To avoid feeling regretful or nervous about what would happen to me now that Chase was gone. I gave myself a pep talk that deflected all responsibility and instead channeled the anger I had buried for some time. "He was the one who prevented me from making money. *He* kept my things at his place and denied me access. *He* created a dependable reason for me to always come back. *He* wanted to play this stupid game with me and Alli—I never wanted any of this!"

Yet the biggest thing of all was that it could have easily been *her* in the car that night. It felt like bitter poison sitting in my throat as I admitted it—oh, how I wished it were Alli! But it wasn't.

Chase's parents came and got the car—after knocking on the door for an hour because I didn't realize they were there. I did my makeup, hair in a towel, while they packed up his townhouse, and when they noticed how spun out I was, they politely asked me to leave. I remember trying to hand Chase's mom the keys to his car. Rummaging around in my purse, fingers trembling, I kept grabbing syringes instead of the keys carelessly flung in there.

I never made a deal with the police; I didn't comply with their snitch contract. I agreed only so I could get out of being arrested that night, and now—I was running. And I was on the run until they found me at Jessie's house exactly one month later.

I think she told the police I was staying with her. She was probably done with my games and the constant threat to her family. She was done with me using her as a safe house. It made her home the exact opposite of safe.

"Ashley Chesney?" the officer asked inquisitively. As if they didn't know. "This is a warrant for your arrest. Please put your hands behind your back."

I was just about to get in the shower, and I had just done a dose, and out of all things, I asked the police, "Can I at least smoke a cigarette?"

Looking back now, I can think of a hundred other things I should have asked to do before going to jail. Like putting on some warmer clothes because the holding cells were freezing, hugging Jessie's little son for the last time, putting my feet on the grass, but no—I wanted to smoke a Newport 100.

***

As I sat for a third time on the cold metal chairs in Cobb County's intake room, I thought back to the first time I was there. I had accumulated an array of sixteen drug felonies. I recounted most of my story to my lawyer, and when I began to describe what happened in Missouri, my lawyer paused.

I had never been in a courtroom for a full hearing, and I was conditioned to what street life taught me. All I knew was that I wasn't supposed to talk to cops, give up information, or work a deal. Trust no one. I didn't understand at the time that my lawyer was trying to help me, and she was spot on.

Upon hearing my fragmented, minimally detailed description of what happened to me before coming to Georgia, she said the phrase I had never heard: *human trafficking*. She told me I was a victim of this crime, and although my memory is foggy, I remember protesting. I was uneducated and fearful about admitting something like that had happened to me—what would happen if I agreed with her? An admission might open a door I was not ready to step through. Would I have to testify? Give names? I wasn't a victim—I was a drug dealer. I was so convinced of this hard street persona I had created. Hardened individuals are not victims; they are invincible.

But how false that narrative was. Clearly, my invincibility had worn off as I sat there in handcuffs, unwilling to adopt the idea that I may have been trafficked.

CHAPTER 10

***

Dr. Bessel van der Kolk writes:

> As we will see, finding words to describe what has
> happened to you can be transformative, but it does not
> always abolish flashbacks or improve concentration,
> stimulate vital involvement in your life or reduce
> hypersensitivity to disappointments and perceived
> injuries.[1]

For much of my life, I lived in a dual reality. Much of it looked like trying to put on a beautiful act that proclaimed, "Everything is just fine here," when I was so, so lost. I was a liar, a manipulator, and taking off my clothes for money. The stage was pretty and glamorous, while my reality was dark, isolating, and highly addictive. In more recent times, I have encountered this dual reality again, the temptation to be something I am not—only now my reality is safe and secure. I live in the routine normality of the present alongside my harrowing and ever-present past. The whispers just come back sometimes.

I often say to the people who have witnessed my journey *and* my rising that I wish my past did not take up so much space in my present. This is a collective reality for many survivors. Healing is never the linear line that everyone hopes it is. Onlookers assume how our lives *should be* after leaving "the life," but sadly, it is not a steady climb of higher trajectory. It is a fight, like someone free-climbing without a harness. Clawing their fingers into the side of the rock, grasping for anything to hold them afloat and

---

[1] Bessel van der Kolk, *The Body Keeps the Score: Brain, Mind, and Body in the Healing of Trauma* (New York: Penguin Publishing Group, 2015), 196.

secure their footing. It is a constant shedding of old behaviors, societal ideals, and devastating baggage that we were never meant to carry. You can be rescued by God from your Egypt. And still forget how bad it truly was.

There are chunks of my life that soar upward in leaps and bounds. Then on other days, I wake up and I'm flung backward. I might be watching a movie, going for a walk, or taking a shower, and *snap*. In an instant, I am transported back to 1999 as a memory appears, and that upward climb to healing drops back down into recovery. I teleport. I time travel.

Yet I believe my resiliency, or "bounce back" as I like to call it, has certainly swelled in capacity. I do not suffer from flashbacks like I once did. I simply have memories, and when they come up, I welcome them. I have learned to ask God why the memory resurfaced, and then I move on. This is growth. But simply put, it isn't a straight line. Healing looks a lot more like a heartbeat monitor that ebbs and flows, up and down. But the peaks and drops get less and less dramatic, and eventually I level out.

***

I sat in Cobb County Jail for almost a year waiting to go to prison. The first three months I slept. A lot. I had some catching up to do.

Thankfully for me, Cobb County Jail is an exceptionally boring place that rarely takes any of its captives outside. They do not offer classes, and I sure as hell didn't have anybody coming to visit me. So there wasn't much to do but sleep, eat, and read.

Speaking of eating, I was coming off a drug that stole my sleep, my hunger, and my peace. I was starving *and* a vegetarian, which made me a very poor candidate for jail. Out of pure desperation,

I managed to choke down some of the semi-edible foods the jail served. Some people can get what they call "store" or commissary every week, which is a process where loved ones send money or place funds on the "books" so those people can buy food. But my family didn't support me. Not yet, anyway. At the time, they weren't even talking to me. They were angry—and so *relieved* that I was in jail and not dead somewhere on the streets.

Every day for lunch we received two bologna-and-cheese sandwiches. Once in a while, heaven would open and we'd get PB&J, but usually it was bologna. Cobb County loved bologna. We had boiled bologna for breakfast, bologna sandwiches for lunch, and fried bologna on our tray for "supper." So gross.

I began asking everybody in my dorm if they were going to eat their sandwiches, and I accepted whatever they were willing to share. Taking two pieces of white bread (eighty-six the bologna), adding mayo and a square piece of "cheese" that was more like plastic, sticking some pretzels inside (for crunch, obviously), and *voilà*—my signature sandwich was born. I ate nearly ten of these sandwiches a day because I was insatiable.

Two women about my mom's age slept in my vicinity. Ms. Kim and Ms. Angela. Ms. Kim was kind and soft spoken as she told me about her family and how they spent summers in Michigan and winters in Florida. She used to have these vividly detailed dreams—or "visions" as she called them—and was always writing them down. She had a brain that remembered dates, times, and detailed imagery. I liked to listen to her, but as I still hadn't let go of my street persona, I kept her at a distance.

She talked about her family as I waited alone and not a single one of my people, my street "family," came to visit me. When I used the phone and called my friends, I could hear it in their voices—they were high and it made me angry. When I called and they didn't answer *because* they were high, that made me angry too. I would stomp up the stairs to my bunk, cause a scene, draw attention to myself. I cussed people out waiting in line for the shower, inserted myself in confrontations, and believed I was justified in doing so. I was a hot mess. And Ms. Kim showed up, loving me in spite of myself.

Ms. Angela was more reserved at first, likely because she was heartbroken. I think she was wrongly accused, and her beautiful family felt torn apart. She and I shared family pictures and stories and joked that I was going to marry her son when I got out. We talked about her niece, who was just a toddler then, and the days Ms. Angela used to get to spend with her. We discussed all the fun activities we would do together if only the walls around us toppled down.

The ironic thing about Ms. Angela is that she was doing jail ministry *before* this happened. She was coming from the outside world to enter the jail and work with the ladies. One day she told me, "I was doing jail ministry, and I told God, 'Please use me in any way You see fit.' I sincerely meant it at the time, but be careful what you pray for." Here she now sat on the inside, with a more direct line to these women than she had ever envisioned. She was mad at God at first—this was not the way she wanted to resolve the issue. Yet He specifically chose her for this task, and she answered. She did what she was called to do and began ministering to women who needed her desperately. One of those desperate women was me.

***

One day my name was called for visitation.

It was Jessie. As I sat looking at her from behind a computer screen, I realized once more that our friendship was over. I could already hear it in the made-up stories, the paranoia, that she was high.

"Your car was stolen," she said offhandedly and then quickly recited a string of rambling lies, backpedaling how she knew such information and defending her non-involvement. "Oh yeah, and all your stuff is in a storage unit."

"Wait," I said, pressing the brakes on her series of unfortunate events. "My car was stolen?"

"Yep, and I've been talking to your mom about the storage unit," she replied. "Because, just so you know—if you get out, you're not welcome at my house anymore."

I don't know why it hurt so badly. It wasn't necessarily Jessie or even that particular conversation. I'd known our friendship was over for quite some time, but I think it hurt because of the loneliness. It was the white cement walls and the metal clanging doors surrounding me. It was the loss of friends who weren't really friends. Grieving the loss of people who were actually just sick. Just a bunch of drug addicts, out to get their piece of the pie. It was the fact that I was most likely going to prison. It was that everything I ever owned up to this point had been stolen—for the second time. Night after night I'd taken my clothes off for money, done things I didn't want to do, all for material goods. And poof. Just like that. All of it—gone again. My reputation was tarnished, and nobody was standing in my court.

After Jessie's visit, I went back upstairs to my bunk, stood pressing my back against the wall, and then sunk to the floor sobbing.

Ms. Kim and Ms. Angela sat with me in my grief. They held me, giving me two giant hugs, which I needed more than I knew at the time. I thought, *I can't remember the last time somebody hugged me.* I'd been living in an alternate universe where the only time somebody touched me was for sex. These hugs were full of love. They were liquid light.

That moment, something released within me.

Through the tears, I let go of the pretending, the needing to be tough, and the drugs. I let go of the people I had known and my life out there on the streets. I had nothing left to prove, and I didn't have to maintain this act any longer. I let go of the need to protect my weakness—I wasn't big, bad, or strong. I came to the end of myself.

Later that night, as I sat on the edge of Ms. Angela's bed eating a PB&J taco (tortilla + peanut butter + jelly = delish!), she talked to me about Jesus.

This, of course, was nothing new to me. A lot of people had told me about God, reciting the Jesus story to me. I'd even witnessed how God showed up for some of those believing people—but He never showed up for me.

There was nothing different about the way Ms. Angela talked about Jesus versus the times I had heard about Him before. However, *I* was different this time. *I* was in a place to receive what she was saying.

Either Jesus was who she said He was, and my life would get better.

Or she was lying, and my life would stay the same.

I had nothing to lose. I was sitting in a dirty jail cell with nothing but a prison sentence hanging over my head. She and I turned toward the stark wall, and she held my hand and we prayed together as I gave my life to Christ. And God began to put my life back together, brick by brick, as if I were one of those white walls sitting in front of me.

***

Ms. Angela fed me spiritually and physically. She was so sweet, and every week on store day, she would buy me the kind of cookies I loved. They were like off-brand Oreos. "Duplex cookies," we called them. Their icing was straight confectioner's sugar. Too sweet. Fake sweet. And I loved them.

She ran a Bible study every day with some of the other women in my dorm, and I took notes, asked questions, had a strong hunger to learn. My Bible constantly lay open on my bunk. I was laser focused, taking all of it in. It was like the words on the pages were illuminated. I didn't want to read anything else. I wanted to know what God had to say.

Little did I know, as I sat poring over my Good News Translation Bible, God was doing more work in my family back home. My brother had just gotten baptized at my cousin's church, and my mom had suffered a heart-wrenching breakup of a seven-year relationship, which eventually led her to meet Jesus for herself—and to meet my stepdad, Zeke, who is an amazing man of God.

God was pursuing my entire family. It didn't matter that three thousand miles separated us from each other. He was setting up a family of believers for me to come home to.

I think that if I hadn't found Him during that year in the county jail, prison would have been wildly different. A much darker place. But because of Him, prison became my rescue. Jesus saved my life, and prison...it set me free.

CHAPTER 11

As a prisoner for the Lord, then, I urge you to live a life worthy
of the calling you have received.

—EPHESIANS 4:1 (NIV)

Like Paul in the Bible, I was in prison, but also like Paul, I was content.

Sure, I was not wrongly accused or incarcerated for my faith. More or less I was guilty, deserving of my sentence. "This is punishment," said the Georgia Department of Corrections. Yet it didn't feel like punishment because I had a goal. A goal to learn as much as I could about God. Who is He? What is His true nature? His character? And who does He say I am? Prison was not a place where chains felt heavy. Prison is where I learned to worship.

Going through diagnostics, I was told I'd be sent to Pulaski, a large maximum-security prison, for two reasons: I was a vegetarian and they were the only prison that supported that kind of dietary restriction, and my security level was high. At Pulaski I would be surrounded by serious offenders and women with life sentences.

Yet I didn't end up at Pulaski but at Whitworth—this tiny prison for women who held shorter sentences. Whitworth was considered a kiddie camp. Lots of short-timers, with the majority of women working outside details. Every day they would leave the prison to go out and weed-eat the parks in the neighboring cities and counties. I was one of the longest-standing inmates there, instead of the other way around. The system sent me to a place I technically shouldn't have been.

Along with my heightened security level and starched brown uniform, I had God as I stepped into Whitworth Women's Facility. I walked every single day with Jesus, guided by a desire to know Him. Of course, I saw some pretty terrible things. I mean, it was a prison. But fights, drama, stealing, violence, and all the usual things that take place inside institutions rarely affected me personally. I walked with favor inside. It took me a while to get my act right, but about a year into my sentence, I adjusted.

My dad and I built a relationship over a phone with a cord connected to the wall. I called home every Wednesday and Sunday night. I began working for the deputy warden on an art detail—the only one in the state of Georgia. This meant I got to paint every day, take classes, and study. When I finally got home to California, a friend joked, "Ash, you didn't go to prison. You went to Bible college." I believe I was on assignment, and God used me. Whatever dorm I was placed in, I made it my mission to make a difference there. Especially for the new girls. I know when I first arrived, I just wanted somebody to be nice to me. Someone to show me what to do, what was expected, what the silent "rules" were, the culture. So that's what I tried to do for them.

During my imprisonment, I had a thirst to know Jesus. I sought Him—I had to, if I wanted any sense of peace. I didn't know when my end date was, but knowing Jesus was enough to keep that uncertainty at bay. I learned how to thrive, no matter where I laid my head. That skill might have started out of survival on the streets, but I got to exercise it while in confinement. Despite the barriers, boundaries, restrictions, and disappointments, I was with Jesus. I knew Jesus. I was safe. I was okay.

Until I wasn't okay, and my safety was compromised yet again. A lieutenant abused his power. I wasn't the only one this officer targeted—but I was the last. For the first time in my life, I used my voice.

Sexual abuse—rape, to be specific—is not "trafficking," yet all abusers share similar characteristics. In prison there are multiple hierarchies: between officers and between inmates. I am not saying that all correctional officers or law enforcement are bad people. This is not a sweeping generalization, and I do not want to categorize anybody. In my experience, not all correctional officers view incarcerated people as criminals or try to treat them as less than human. Mutual respect *does* exist. Unfortunately, it is seen far less often. What I saw more of was a third hierarchy that existed between officers and inmates, with the inmates residing at the bottom where they were seen as trash, below any person in a blue uniform.

Unless, of course, you had an in. And just like on the streets, there's always a way in. Everything has a price. A secret exchange, in which "I'll do this for you; you do this for me" is apparent. Nothing is ever for free. This lieutenant was a master manipulator. Just like a trafficker, he had a system, a tactic, and he handpicked his prey. He was an unsafe person dressed up in a fancy uniform, with a fancy title, where he exercised his authority to get what he wanted.

I was afraid to go to sleep, because some nights I would wake up to him watching me as he patrolled the dorm. He was under investigation frequently and would get periods of suspension, but when I least expected it, there he was back on duty. His eyes would lock with mine; I would quickly glance away trying to find something, anything, to focus on other than his eyes. Usually I just looked at my feet. But staring down at my black shiny boots, I could still *feel* him. On the yard or in the dorms, staring in his predatory way, my heart beating so loudly that I was afraid he could hear it.

With nowhere to go, confined within the walls of prison, I felt trapped. I couldn't trust those on his side, and those on my side were jealous. They saw it as a privilege; I was getting something they weren't. Oh, how little they knew about this arrangement. I wasn't gaining anything special. I had been here before. "Do this because I say so, and keep your mouth shut because nobody is going to believe you anyway." I dealt with the trauma response alone—until finally God showed up for me. And my truth was validated.

And God *kept* showing up for me. I sat in prison for two years on a probation violation waiting to go to court for the big charges with Chase. Nothing seemed to be moving. The final time I was transported to Cobb County for my court date, I sat there in dismay as the judge gave me a fifteen-do-seven sentence, meaning I would serve a portion of the seven years in prison and serve the rest on parole/probation until the fifteen-year mark was complete.

Despite the unexpected length of the sentence, the judge erased my drug trafficking charge. He reduced it all the way down to simple possession charges. But I knew who *really* reduced my charges: God, which is just like Him—to show up in miraculous ways. Even my lawyer was surprised.

God also eliminated all my restitution. He is *that* sweet. Many girls I knew were sitting in prison with the same charges I had but with fines and restitution equaling over $300,000. I knew if I just remained faithful to the season I was in, then God's favor would rain down. That perfectly describes my prison experience. I was barely twenty-four years old and didn't know when I was going home, but I kept my head up and pretended I did. I pretended I could see a horizon somewhere.

I was, however, still disappointed. I had hoped to be released. I'd put in the work those last two years, made giant strides in my healing that I wanted to bring home with me and show off. Today I recognize that I wasn't ready, and I'm thankful God saw it that way as well. It was a maturation issue, and He wasn't done with His careful refining process.

When I got back to Whitworth from the county jail, two friends threw me a party. They decorated the wall above my top bunk with magazine cutouts and hand-drawn signs. They cooked for me and even made a cake. Yes, it's hard to rest in the unknown of release. It's hard to sit in your consequences, crying out, "How long, God?" But people loved me through it and I loved them back. I had *real* friends in prison and I was okay.

When my time was extended, I wrote in my journal:

I don't know how long You'll have me wait, Lord, but I'm willing to do what You say. I just have two requests when I get out, whenever that may be. I want to work with special needs kids (specifically children with autism), and I want to help girls coming out of the sex trade.

***

In May 2016, while I was running on the treadmill (one of maybe three times we were actually allowed to use workout equipment), God spoke to me.

I had some rap song blasting in my ears, and I was immediately catapulted back to life in the strip clubs. Songs have a tendency to do that to me, and I have to be careful what I listen to. That particular day, the flashback sent my thoughts spiraling downward. Romanticizing the time when I used to dance. I felt torn. I wanted to be obedient to the will of God, for all that He had planned for my life, which meant I knew going back to a strip club was not on the agenda. But it was hard to fully trust Him. Would He really provide for me? Even though I knew Jesus, I still felt this tug back to the darkness, like it was calling to me. Honestly, I have a very good understanding of what Paul meant in the book of Romans when he said, "I do what I don't want to do."

The pull to re-enter "the life" is real for many survivors. I felt the enemy, right then and there. For many years as I spun my own web, the devil wasn't worried about me because I'd made his job easy. I was in bad enough shape on my own. But now as the Lord was on the brink of giving me a ministry, the devil quietly whispered how quickly and easily I could get money once I was out. How I could work for just a weekend and have everything I needed. He reminded me how exciting it was to be validated and desired like I once was. That using my body for profit was something I was good at.

I could feel my feet hit the treadmill. It was like I was trying to run faster to beat the intrusive thoughts that were not my own.

All of a sudden, calming peace washed over me. It cleared away the lies I had just entertained and replaced them with truth. I realized that maybe *part* of the pull back to that lifestyle wasn't actually from Satan at all—but from God. I didn't hear some booming voice out of heaven, but God did speak to my heart, and this is what He said: "Why don't you go into the clubs and tell them about Me?"

What? I thought. *Tell a bunch of strippers about Jesus?*

I didn't know if that would work, but if it was God's assignment for me, I knew it *would* work. I wasn't going to fail. I'd been exactly where those girls were, and I knew the grittiness that went on in their world—I could help them. Slowly I began to realize maybe the idea wasn't crazy. Maybe I had a pull to the streets because God wanted to send me back there, to go in the clubs, to walk the boulevard, and to let His glory shine through.

This whole time I'd been praying for an expected end. That God would give me something tangible to hold on to. I'd heard about a lot of ministries, loved what they were doing, and wanted to get involved, but nothing felt specifically *mine*. Nothing felt like it was my assignment or purpose. What about mission trips to Africa or the Dominican Republic? What about adoption? What about working with special needs kids?

But that day in the prison gym, I realized, "*This* I can do." I could get out and tell these girls about Jesus. And even if I helped just one person, that would be okay. I just wanted to do what God wanted me to do.

***

Several years later, that memory on the treadmill came flooding over me as I prepared to speak to a group of law enforcement agencies at the California Lottery building in Sacramento. I was with Carissa Phelps from the Runaway Girl team; our training event was the next day.

I said to Carissa, "Even if I just help one person, this work will be worth it."

She looked at me and replied, "That's what I'm titling your slides. 'Just one person.'"

And from then on, that was my statement. I've used it in multiple speaking engagements as I remind those who are doing direct service work that they *are* making a difference, even if it's just one person.

CHAPTER 12

It took me quite a long time to develop a voice,
and now that I have it, I am not going to be silent.

—MADELEINE ALBRIGHT

While incarcerated, I took every class offered in an attempt to heal. Experiencing God, Highway to Heaven, Celebrate Recovery. I went to AA, attended church on the weekends, and sat in mental health groups with a trauma therapy dog. During my final year at Whitworth, I was selected for Kairos: a weekend "retreat" led by mentors and leaders who are trying to meet the needs of incarcerated women.

One of the beautiful things about Kairos is all the mail. They get outside people involved with prayer and letter writing, and on the last day, they laid out all these pieces of mail for us to see. Prayer chains. Hundreds of prayers for us. Brightly colored paper all interlaced and connected together like the countdown-to-Christmas chains we made in kindergarten, except these went on for what seemed like miles. Each one with a prayer written on it. I could not believe that many people cared for *me*. People I had never even met. It touched something deep inside my soul, awakening a part of me that I had let collect dust. The knowing, and believing, that I could be loved like that. That I was deserving of love like that. I think that was the mission of the entire Kairos weekend—for us to feel real *agape* love.

For anybody reading this who has ever been involved in a prison ministry, thank you. The people who came faithfully every week to run classes with us became pillars in my life. They became mentors, like family.

***

A church called Lighthouse Ministries used to come to the prison. During one of the services, a pastor we called Mr. Lonnie pulled me aside and told me he had a message for me.

Why me? I thought. I was in a room full of inmates.

"The Lord is going to use you in a mighty way," he said. "If you continue to follow Him."

I thought about it. *If I continue to follow God?* I realized it was up to me. Following God was a choice.

He walked away joking about my tattooed arm and all the colors, and I didn't see him again—until two years later, when I stepped into a makeshift prison classroom and sat down in a blue plastic chair. It was my first night of Overcomers, a workbook-based class focused on addiction recovery and the gospel, and in walked Mr. Lonnie. I immediately remembered the day he'd pulled me aside, and for the remainder of the class, I thought about the words he'd spoken over me. Was that just something he'd said in the moment? Something he told hundreds of incarcerated girls as they came and went through prison doors? Or was that message specifically for me?

When the class ended, he stopped me. "I remember you! I saw your arm!"

I smiled at him, afraid to ask if that was all he remembered.

But then he said, "I said something to you a long time ago. Do you remember? Praise God you're still here!"

"I remember," I replied.

It meant so much to me that *he* remembered. Not just that he remembered my face (my arm, in this case), but the words he'd said to me. It solidified within me that what he'd said wasn't just a churchy, generalized phrase he used as he passed through prisons—it was real. A message from God. That was scary and exciting all at the same time.

I'd been in prison for years at this point, and I was starting to feel somewhat complacent. I'd been going about the motions, a routine, in my relationship with God, but that night seeing Mr. Lonnie again sparked something inside me. I *felt* Him—the Holy Spirit moving throughout the room, and He relit the fire within me. I could sense that I was going home soon. That my time was almost here. The love of God poured into me, and I felt overwhelmed and truly in love with Him. That He could use something so simple to get my attention. I had never experienced someone speaking over my life that way—and then God distinctly backing it up two years later. I held on to that feeling tightly.

One month later, I got a TPM (tentative projected month) backdated for February 2017. I would have been released immediately, but I'm from California so my interstate compact took three months to finalize. Exactly four months after the night I saw Mr. Lonnie, I was on my way home.

***

At the beginning of my sentence, when I thought about the time I'd spent in "the life," I used to feel discouraged. Thinking about all the time I wasted, out on the streets and inside the walls of confinement. I was twenty-two when I got arrested and twenty-six when I got home, yet God refined me in the fire. He told me one day, "I will restore the years the locusts have eaten" (Joel 2:25), and He showed me who I am in Him—the person He's always intended me to be. Prison was not what I envisioned for my life growing up. However, if given the chance, I would do it all over again, every single day, all four years, because of what it's done for me and my family. I was released on June 21, 2017.

It was scary and exciting knowing I was going home. Terrified and overjoyed. Worried I would never have friends like the ones I had in prison—praying, giving, loving women who walked with each other through some deep struggles. I was one of the few ladies without children. Most of them were mothers, wives, daughters, without their families.

Like Mr. Lonnie brought to light, following God is a choice. God, in all of His sweetness, doesn't *make* us do anything. We get to choose. In prison being sober was a choice. A choice I made after giving my life to Christ. I am so thankful you don't have to come to God cleaned up. I never would've made it. I came to Him in a jail cell, thinking I was a drug-addicted stripper. I didn't know I was His precious daughter and a trafficking survivor, loved and fully known. I had chosen salvation—but to truly walk with God? I made some slips in the beginning, and walking in disobedience is also a choice. And man, is it painful. During those times, I would feel the absence of God's presence, and it felt like the Holy Spirit was pounding on my chest, saying, "Do not trade eternal blessings for something temporary." I needed those slips, just as I needed the Spirit to remind me who I was. It was those setbacks that propelled me forward and allowed me to make the decision to follow God wholeheartedly. I didn't want to break my family's heart anymore, but more importantly, I did not want to break God's heart anymore.

Shortly before my release, I wrote in my journal, *The old me is dead.* In deep reflection, I was meditating on the thought that Christ made me a new creation—while in confinement. I will never stop being in awe of God and His ways. I sat awaiting release and I was *new*, like the springtime when the trees bring forth new growth on top of the old, on top of the dead and the rot. I wondered who I would be when I was on the other side of captivity. And suddenly felt a prick of sadness. I had grown up and out of the rubble of my old lives, my old personas, and the people and things I cared for. I knew and trusted God would restore what I had lost, yet I never thought I would be here. That I would have to go through *this*. Prison was not what I had anticipated. For years of my life to be taken, sucked away, in order for me to get to be the person I am today.

I remember the sense of heaviness resting on my chest as I looked around the room. The thought occurred to me that this was probably the last time I would ever see these people. I looked bunk to bunk, recounting moments with each of these women, and something sharp poked at my heart.

I was different now. I could love hard and my spirit was clean. My head was no longer foggy and clogged up by chemicals, so I no longer forgot things. I remembered them. I formed real friendships in prison, some of the deepest, and then we broke apart and *poof.* Gone. I didn't hear from them, and I never saw them again.

Many of the women I called my friends while incarcerated went back to their old selves. The few who did contact me seemed like different people. I no longer knew them. The monster had already changed them. Just like that. It's like they didn't have a fighting chance. They tried to do "good" for a while, but their environment, their families, and all of their surroundings led them back to the life of destruction. For every year I was locked up, and for every year I have been home, a girl I once called my friend has died. She went back to the life of addiction, and she wound up dead or lost.

I do not want to ever revert back to the person I once was.

I actually can't do it. It's impossible.

I penned the closing line in my journal entry: *The old me is dead. I buried her.*

CHAPTER 13

Return home and tell how much God has done for you.

—LUKE 8:39 (NIV)

As I walked out of Whitworth Women's Facility in my bright green starched button-down shirt, box-like Dickies pants, and black ballet flats, my hands were shaking. I had imagined this day for years, and now that it was here, it didn't seem real.

I hugged my mom and began to cry. This was the first time in years I was able to hug her without being monitored, without a time cap. I didn't want to let go. First we went and ate pancakes. Then she asked, "How about we get you a new outfit? Does that sound good?"

It did sound good, but at the strip mall I panicked when I saw men without correctional uniforms. My stomach tied itself in knots until I felt sick. Exposed. I kept trying to cover myself up. Crossing my arms. Concealing myself. I also felt a rush of anger.

I changed in the privacy of the dressing room and walked right out of the store.

I needed a minute.

***

My family helped me. Not everybody gets that chance, and trust me—I understand how truly fortunate I am. Sometimes I wonder if I would be where I am today, if I would have made it, without the love and support I received upon release. The family I didn't choose, but the family I was given. The cards I was dealt. Why me? Why was I so lucky? I came home to a house without drug use or violence. To a family who wanted to go to church on Sunday, and go hiking, and had collected clothes and toiletries and all kinds of goodies for me *for years*. I had nothing walking out of prison. And then I had everything.

They were kind to me when I couldn't make decisions. When I didn't know what I wanted for dinner or when I cried for hours because there were too many choices in my closet. I know it sounds silly, but when every choice is made for you for years, it is overwhelming when the power to choose suddenly lands in your hands. When my mom and I went to the Cheesecake Factory the day of my release, I had a meltdown at the table. They have one of the largest menus probably in the world, and it was easier when somebody told me what to eat.

Three months after coming home, I got a job. Also three months after coming home, I jumped fifteen feet off a balcony and broke my leg. A picture-perfect metaphor for what life felt like at the time. Risky. Exciting. Painful. The job I had prayed for arrived in my lap, and I began working for a company that provides services and support for children with developmental disabilities, autism spectrum disorders, and behavioral challenges in schools and at home. I fell in love with these kiddos and their families. And as it turned out, they loved me too and I was good at my job! I ended up becoming a registered behavior technician through the state of California. I worked in the schools mainly with elementary-aged kids and provided in-home services after school to some of my learners. I was enamored with this work and forever grateful my company gave me the chance to do not just a job—but a job I loved.

***

I was at a Celebrate Recovery meeting one Friday night when a woman named Sharon approached me.

"I don't know if this means anything to you," she said, "but God told me to talk to you about human trafficking."

I just stared at her. My other dream, my other prayer, the vision on the treadmill, and my past all flashed through my head. That was the one part of my story I wasn't ready to share. I hadn't told anybody. Yet here Sharon was standing in front of me.

"I feel called to do some type of ministry with girls on the streets," she said.

Holding back tears, I asked, "How can I help?"

Later as I walked away, I whispered silently, "Thank You, Jesus."

God hears us. In my own life, His timing has never been what I thought it was going to be, but, of course, it's perfect. Meeting Sharon and doing outreach was the opening I needed for Him to come burst down the door for me, so I could start working in the anti-human trafficking movement.

Sharon called her ministry Wings, and her heart to take action was incessant. We didn't do everything perfectly, but we did it. We began collecting gift bags and passing them out in areas known for exploitation in Salinas, California. We'd go out in the middle of the night and have no idea what we were doing. Just two women alone on a mission from God. Sometimes we would see women and often we wouldn't see anybody. At the time, we didn't understand the value of building rapport with the women we saw. We handed out gift bags through the car window, never venturing out onto the street ourselves. I now understand this created a barrier that separated us from them. I just wanted these girls to know they were loved, that I had been where they were, but I couldn't really communicate those words from the safety of a vehicle.

One day Sharon presented me with a book called *Runaway Girl* by Carissa Phelps.[1] I hadn't told Sharon my whole story, just bits and pieces, claiming I'd been involved in the commercial sex industry. But trafficking? At the time, I still wasn't sure that was really what happened to me. Sharon met Carissa at a speaking event and had her sign a copy of her book to me.

"I have a friend who just came out of the life," she explained.

As I read Carissa's story, I finally realized the truth. "Oh my gosh. This *is* what happened to me." It was the first time I fully identified with being a trafficking survivor. Flashbacks from my lawyer in Georgia appeared. This book in my hand made me curious to learn more.

Trafficking. I found the word so aversive, like it wasn't mine to claim. Why was everybody so comfortable with the idea? I had pushed it away for so long, and I guess I wasn't ready to look at

---

[1] Penguin Books (2012).

it, take it apart, really dissect it, and figure out where it fit in my timeline. As I learned more, God slowly revealed a hardship in my life that He would turn to be the greatest strength. The revealing of this truth required a constant shedding of old layers, old skin, and the Lord must have known that now, finally, I was ready to peel them back. What was hidden inside of me slowly made its way to the surface, and I became ready to do the healing work.

***

When I think about dates in my life, I picture little birthday cakes with the months written on them. That is how my first-grade teacher presented the idea of months to us. She stuck twelve paper birthday cakes on the wall, six months on the left and six on the right, and to this day, my brain still organizes months according to cakes.

After high school, my months fragmented. As the years passed, memories slowly began to return to me until I could form the timeline of this book. In the course of writing it, I discovered more. Not just dates, but clarity moments and introspective reasoning as to why the brain stores memories the way it does, only to come to a completely new conclusion about an event years later. That is how much of my trauma has worked. I felt a certain way about the experience in the beginning, but when God decided it was time for me to heal, I began digging and found something completely new. In most cases, the new thing was about my safety, perspective, and His presence. I began to walk through painful memories by adding Jesus to them, and slowly I pieced together the shattered parts of my life.

After I'd been home for a year, I walked into a room full of people and took my seat—alone, brave—at an event called Gospel and Justice, hosted by a local church. A man named Joshua

Ryan Butler talked about foster youth and human trafficking in the Seattle area where he lived. The breakout session I chose to attend that afternoon was focused locally. It was one of the most well-attended sessions of the day, and the room was crowded and awkwardly quiet.

I watched as a handful of people stood up and gave their presentation—they had no idea how they would impact my life going forward. Ginger Coakley, cofounder and executive director for Edens Glory. Kim Hernandez, a San Bernardino police detective. Michael Aspland, retired law enforcement from Monterey. Felicia George, vice president of the organization I now work for.

At the time, Mike had a desire to build a home for sex trafficking survivors. "God spoke to me on an airplane," he said. "He told me to build a home for trafficked women in Carmel Valley, California. With horses."

If you know the area, you know this was no small "ask" God presented before him.

Currently, Monterey County has zero resources available for victims of human trafficking who are seeking residential care. This lack includes crisis intervention and temporary shelters. There is virtually nothing. As I listened to these people speak, I was surprised and intrigued to realize they had the same calling I did. This was what I was looking for.

Felicia George had been doing human trafficking education in the schools for many years. Ginger and Annie, her cofounder, ran a successful home in Illinois for survivors, and the way they talked about it, I wanted to jump on a plane and immediately start serving there.

As I listened to Mike and Kim speak, I felt slightly put off by the fact that two law enforcement officers were standing in front of me, yet they spoke about something I wanted to get involved with too. I heard the kindness in Kim's voice; she had worked undercover and was deeply ingrained in the women's lives on the streets. She spoke as if they were her daughters. This was the kind of shift I needed. Only God could present me with two Jesus-loving police officers and change my thinking about working with law enforcement.

After the presentation, I approached the group, mainly just wanting to thank Kim. Thank her for treating girls like me with dignity. I wanted her to know that by doing that for *them*, somehow it was doing it for me. I had never experienced love like that on the streets, but it was comforting to know somebody like her existed. She didn't see women like me as garbage but as quite the opposite.

"I am a survivor," I said. "I'm from Monterey County. How can I help?"

Mike approached me. "I have three daughters your age," he said with tears streaming down his cheeks. He said I broke his heart that day, and it was all the fire he needed. From that day, Set Free Monterey Bay was born: the ministry I currently work for that serves adult women who have been sexually trafficked.

***

Starting a grassroots organization is tough work.

We had a lot of learning curves, including the pandemic, but you know what? We're still standing. We have assisted multiple survivors to safety and contribute to survivor needs by supporting therapeutic services. We have numerous community partners and have established mentoring services with the residents at other safe houses. As an organization, we've entered a legal partnership with Edens Glory, the home in Illinois. This means that one day we, too, will have a residential program. A restoration home of our own. I long for the day we will get to pour into these women over a two-year period and watch them obtain a restored life, just like I have.

Working in the field of human trafficking as a survivor has given me the space to step into generous opportunities. As the program coordinator for Set Free Monterey Bay, I've spoken at many events and trainings. I was the keynote speaker for the 2020 Monterey County Human Trafficking Symposium, and I've attended survivor retreats and wilderness trips.

At one of those retreats in the Santa Cruz Mountains, in walked Carissa Phelps. I did this strange thing that people do when they see celebrities. I managed to regain my composure and tried not to cry. She had *no* idea who I was, but I knew so much about her. She changed the course of my life and didn't even know it. She gave me my voice in this movement, all because she wrote a book and gave me words for what I had experienced on the streets.

Today I get the privilege of calling her my mentor. She continues to amplify my voice in the movement, and she's asked me to speak, present, and train as an expert in the field of sex trafficking. She is the founder of Runaway Girl Inc., a survivor-led organization where she uses her platform to give a platform to others. She is a beautiful example of the expression "passing the torch" as she displays amazing leadership *and* humility, allowing people to see there is room for us all within the movement.

***

Trauma is cunning and powerful. Some days my body reminds me of the past. It shows up in back pain, clenched teeth, tension in my shoulders and feet, heaviness in my chest. All of these signs are marks of activation for me. They ignite the amygdala part of the brain, sending a flight-or-fight response. I managed stress for a long time by simply dissociating. Chunks of time would pass as I ran on autopilot. Today triggering memories no longer haunt me; they take up only a small space. When I feel them coming, I can accept them, yield to them, and *soften*. My natural flight-or-fight response is to freeze; because I could not fight, I learned another way to escape. An easier way, since I am non-confrontational and being assertive is not my strong suit. Leaving my body was something I was pretty good at.

I still have a hard time relaxing, so I practice embodiment. Learning about breath work and movement, doing yoga. These are not things that come naturally for me, and I need to be intentional about them or I won't do them. I have reminders on my fridge, on my bathroom mirror. When my world starts spinning and I find myself going through the motions, I remind myself to do these small things that allow me to rest and settle back home in my body.

My old coping skills no longer serve me. Sure, as humans we have a tendency to fall back into old patterns, and my body does what it knows. But I regroup, reset, and intentionally take a breath. Jesus *died* to set me free. Not half free, or kinda free. *All the way free.* And I can't be free if my body is all bound up inside.

If I want to experience true freedom, I have to put in the work to get there. For me, part of that work means walking through therapy practices like EMDR (Eye Movement Desensitization and Reprocessing, which can help trauma survivors heal through bilateral stimulation), and Internal Family Systems, a practice developed by Richard C. Schwartz that focuses on subpersonalities of different emotions (kind of like the Pixar movie *Inside Out*). IFS therapy addresses memories and the emotional strongholds behind them. In my case, this kind of therapy looks like walking hand in hand with someone I trust. Sometimes walking slowly, sometimes running full speed ahead. She guides me through different activities but allows me to control the pace. She taught me about breath work and singing ancient Hebrew words when my body feels stuck and my soul needs to speak. It means a lot of rewiring of my brain, stopping traumatic brain loops and thought processes, saying goodbye to old neighborhoods I built there and creating new ones.

Coming back into my body has been the most interesting and almost unintentional experience. I didn't know how detached I truly was until I finally arrived home.

Dr. Bessel van der Kolk writes:

> While we all want to move beyond trauma, the part of our brain that is devoted to ensuring our survival (deep below our rational brain) is not very good at denial. Long after a traumatic experience is over, it may reactivate at the slightest hint of danger. It can re-mobilize disturbed brain circuits, and secrete massive amounts of stress hormones. This precipitates unpleasant emotions, intense physical sensations, and impulsive and aggressive actions. These posttraumatic reactions feel incomprehensible and overwhelming. Feeling out of control, survivors of trauma often begin to fear that they are damaged to the core and beyond redemption.[2]

I am not beyond redemption. God has truly given me a redeemed life, exchanging what many would call scandal for a second

---

[2] Van der Kolk, *The Body Keeps the Score.*

chance. I want to leave something as a result of that chance—as a result of my gifted second journey through this life. I refuse to pass through as a taker. I want to be a giver and to bless others in tangible ways.

Today I get to use my experience to benefit others. I am a mentor, a leader, and a friend. Out of a desire to be more than my lived experience, I also became a student. I excel at school, something I never wanted to do. I have authentic relationships. Most importantly with my family. I get to show up in each of these roles fully present and fully sober.

Then came the day I was presented with a new role: wife.

I got married, continued to heal, only to realize I could not stay in that place, and had to walk through the sting of divorce. But I will never look at that relationship as wasted time. Should I have walked down the aisle? No. But that doesn't change the fact that he brought something real and necessary into my life. He showed me relational safety, security, laughter, how to trust another person—a male person. I went from "the life" to prison and then straight to him. I needed a relationship to show me something different, that good men do exist.

Through heartbreak, I learned how to step away from the rigid view I held of God and what life with Him is "supposed" to look like. In the valley of experience, I have found Him in the grey. Life in the grey means there is no pass or fail. It means there is *flexibility*: a curse word to someone who holds control in high regard, as I tried to do for years. Control feels safe, while flexibility feels scary. But experiencing the grey looks like moving away from the need to know the outcome. It is searching for God and *not* finding answers—but finding His presence. As I have practiced living in the grey, I have found Him in the most real way since receiving salvation. God was there with me in the fluid, beautiful, and painful parts of life, and divorce was no exception. He spoke. He comforted me. Sometimes we place judgment on things and try to categorize them as good or bad, and sometimes they are neither. Sometimes they just are.

***

For three years I lived on a tightrope. Each step careful. Only strategic movements that ensured safety.

Tightropes suck up all the air until your life feels suffocating. Constricting. Fear based. The entire time you're up there, you are afraid, wishing you could just reach the end so you could finally take a breath. But when you're *living* on a tightrope, the end never comes, so you just keep holding your breath and sucking in the air until you eventually fall. I thought the tightrope life was what God wanted. I thought I needed to perform, to do.

God instills His Spirit inside our bodies, sharing His incomprehensible power with us—that thought is mind-blowing. But because we can't *see* His miraculous power simmering under the surface, sometimes we bow down and adopt the ways of human institutions and ideologies. We believe we are doing the right thing, but human things are less than the power of God. We can end up with a stronger trust in the things of the world because we can see them, yet they will never serve us like God's best can. And I want God's best.

I am not afraid of suffering. God has done much bigger things than heal shattered hearts. Though I lost a relationship, I gained so much more. I no longer feel trapped in my body. When I stopped having to pretend all the time, my authentic self showed up. I gained *me*. The real me. When I stopped floating away to tolerate all the things I was told I should do versus what I actually wanted, my true self showed up. I gained freedom, strength, and bravery, and I gained the truth about who God says I am. I also gained the knowledge that I made the right choice.

A wise woman once told me that life with God is about movement, joy, and pain. Life is about feeling big feelings, tasting raspberries, feeling your bare feet on the grass, having beautiful sex and deep conversations, and, yes, sometimes feeling crippling grief. But you know what? God doesn't need us to do anything for Him so we can experience those things. That's not what He created us for—to do. He made us *to be*. And to enjoy all that He created, all the while praising Him for who He truly is.

My story is not the same as many of the stories found within the walls of a church. I've had to dismiss what culture and structuralized religion were screaming at me. I've had to pause. Take a step back. Find my inner voice and listen to the Holy Spirit's leading. I believe God ultimately wants me to choose what my soul speaks versus what I was conditioned to believe. Because *that* is who He is.

Enveloped in your glory

But also in a world of hurt (Shadow found me in my grief)

Sounds of the wind

Speak to my soul

Water running downstream

As I steadily climb

Up

Up

Up

***

Recently God once again met me in the wilderness. This time *outside* the walls of confinement.

As I drank in creation on a mountain in Wyoming, I knew I was right where I was supposed to be. I sought His design, the sounds of the wind, gave my full attention to all that surrounded me. With the absence of distraction and the noise of the world gone, God seemed so loud. He met me there in my grief, my anger, my sadness. As I walked through these emotions, I found a stable path—a sure-footed feeling that the joy, freedom, and right standing deserved a place inside of me. My incessant thoughts had been playing on an endless loop in my head, keeping me trapped in the desert wandering around Egypt. I refused to stay in that place anymore, so that day I made a choice. I committed to embracing the suffering, entering a place of healing, with confidence. Knowing God was *right* there, I let go of the need to know the outcome.

I love mornings. Watching the sunrise, my spirit rising with it. A new day. New mercies. Knowing healing is accessible, that we can praise while also weeping. My heart was heavy but full as I walked along the river's edge. Connecting to creation is what has really allowed me to come home to myself, more than connecting with community. Humans can fail, but God never fails me, and He knows what to do to help grieving hearts grow stronger.

He is enough. He's sufficient to meet our needs even when the pit is deep and the obstacle high, when the suffering seems ongoing. It just proves that no matter the circumstance, He is faithful. As Becca Stevens writes:

Mercy takes us from the Wilderness to the gentle
pastures. Mercy is available to everybody. Nobody is
too bad or too good to receive it, that's what gets us
through, that's what gives us hope.[3]

I had to go through many, many seasons with the Lord to
arrive where I am today. To know that love *does* heal. And now
that I am here, all I want to do is what the Lord asks of me. To
help those stuck in the curse of captivity and exploitation. I want
to be whole for their sake, for my sisters around the world who
are still suffering.

The pain and the waiting are not the fun parts of healing, but
combined together they bring forth rising. I don't know if I've
fully risen from the ashes yet. I don't believe I've reached the peak
of my own rising. Most days I feel there is more ascending to do.
More mornings. More fresh days.

***

When I speak with survivors who are faced with walking away
from a life of exploitation, I often ask them, "What is it going to
take to make you stay?" To stay in the healing process until it is
completed.

More often than not, they don't stay—they run. The trauma
speaks more loudly than any words I could possibly say. But my
hope for all victims is that they find their reason. Their reason to
sit in the pain and embrace the waiting. For me, that came when I
found hope—when I found Jesus. Anyone can provide resources
and fulfill our basic needs. In fact, many traffickers accomplish

---

[3] Becca Stevens, *Love Heals* (Nashville: Thomas Nelson, 2017).

this all the time. But what will meet their needs long term? What is going to make them stay in the unknown and pursue healing rather than "the life" and what it provides? Eternal life far outweighs any comfort the world pretends to offer. Personally, I want to experience my rising. So I am committed to stay.

Honestly, over the years I have traveled in circles like I'm on a diabolical carousel. Yet I *finally* found freedom as I gained the tools to battle my demons and win. My world has become a lovely place because I appreciate every moment *not* spent in the grip of the monster. A monster with an attractive face that comes in the form of chemicals. A monster that stole my light. I won't pretend this is easy—I still dream about that monster from time to time. I miss the monster's kiss and how he used to make me feel. The escape he offered. For a while, I thought about getting high and justifying it as my "one last time," just so the world would make sense for a heartbeat or two.

But then that strength returns. It rises up and fights off the enemy. I no longer travel in circles, but I embrace life's curvy roads and hilly terrain, and I know traveling down always leads to going back up.

I wanted the perfect ending, and I know now that it doesn't come. I learned the hard way that we sometimes burn dinner, we say the wrong things, and we trip going up the stairs. My heart has found peace in accepting that the perfect ending never comes this side of heaven. That's where I have landed. I am realizing more and more that I get to step out of perfectionism and into the place of grace. That special spot of less "rigid" and more fluidity. There aren't perfect endings because the endings aren't here yet.

Some stories don't have a clear beginning, middle, and end. That is okay because my story is far from over. I'm no longer striving for it to be perfect...but I'm resting in *not knowing*. And I'm looking in expectation for what's going to happen next.

***

Each time I have shared my story, I have gotten braver. So thank you to the people who heard my story in the beginning and allowed me to slowly reveal all of my truth. Some parts are shameful and not worth remembering. Many memories have resurfaced, and I have the privilege of learning all over again that God is a patient Healer. I am thankful I didn't start working through my story until after I met Him. Many moments of understanding came to me while in prison, where I was safe and unable to reach for many of my comfort vices. In that place of safety, I began to remember some of the darkness. Later, through the process of therapy and even while writing this book, I had many "ah-ha" moments. Most of them were unpleasant, yet I trust God's proper timing, and I know the fact that I'm remembering as much as I am speaks to the confidence He has in *me*, His child. He believes the revealing of my story at this time is appropriate. That I can handle this information as truth, and that I'm ready for more healing to come. *Ready to heal.* Not to cover it up, inject it with chemicals, or push it away. Thank you for allowing me to share God's story. Because that's really whose story this is.

Also, I thank God for allowing me to tell it. For one, there's a sense of safety. When I tell it, I'm the one in control of the story, and I don't have to share every detail, because He is the One who knows it all. And for two, if I am the one who gets to tell the story, it no longer hurts as much. It doesn't have to stay inside me while I try to move on. If I'm the one to tell the story,

I get to try my best to make you, the hearer, laugh instead of having you feel sorry for me. I am no longer a victim. I am a survivor. I am a *thriver*. God took every single dark thing in my life, every single mistake I made, and He flipped it. He turned it completely around for His glory.

I'm not scared anymore. Not if His glory gets to be my narrative.

FINAL THOUGHTS

As I worked on this book, God did something big.

This year, 2021, proved to be a big legislative year for trafficking victims. Several states passed Survivor Relief Acts, and Georgia was no exception. A team of lawyers from Jones Day law firm worked on my case for almost a year. In Georgia they require you to be one year off probation or parole before they grant any type of survivor relief. The argument is that these people would not have committed crimes if not for their exploitative situations and trafficker's control.

I was on parole/probation for eight years.

But then on November 5, 2021, the DA and the judge signed the motion, effective immediately, for early termination of probation and parole. They sent me a handwritten note saying how proud they were of me and that, in one year's time, I could apply for the Survivor Cares Act, which they are 100 percent committed to signing as well. The Cares Act will allow me to have full vacature of my record. This means that one year from now, if somebody looks me up in the system, I will have no criminal charges. As a sixteen-time convicted felon, this is huge. Not only for me, but for every single survivor sister I have ever crossed paths with and mentored. They, too, can receive vacature and relief.

Our judicial system is starting to realize what is actually happening to women, men, and children in our country. Myself included. Change is coming.

ACKNOWLEDGMENTS

Tears immediately formed in my eyes when I began writing this part of the book. There are so many people who contributed to this moment. Some of you crossed my path only for a season, and some of you I hope will be around a lifetime, but each one of you helped me get to where I am today. Thank you.

***

Mom and Dad: Thank you for not giving up. Thank you for showing me tough love but remaining hopeful, allowing me to find my own way. Nobody ever says, "This is going to happen to my kid." I am so thankful for your support and the incredible restoration God has given our family. I want readers to know what truly wonderful parents you both were and are. Thank you for always encouraging my writing, and, Dad, even if you never read this book—I hope you read this part.

To my brother, **Dylan:** I love you more than you will ever know. I dreamed of the day when I could show up as your sister again.

That day is here. Thank you for giving me the chance. I couldn't have released this book without you. Thank you for all you have done in support of this dream. Now you go bury it in the backyard.

Zeke: Thank you for being one of the first men God used to prove to me that not all men are bad. Thank you for also showing my mom who Jesus is.

Ms. Angela: You set the foundation for my entire incarceration. Prison would have been a very different experience if not for you, your obedience, and the way you presented the gospel to me that day. You changed my eternal destiny. How do I thank someone for that kind of gift? I love you with all my heart.

Sharon: Thank you for listening to the Lord. Thank you for speaking about human trafficking, for starting Wings, and for handing me Carissa's book—you cracked open the door I was meant to walk through.

Carissa Phelps: Thank you for writing *Runaway Girl*. Thank you for giving words to what happened to me. Thank you for your mentorship and for sharing your platform. You have taught me so much. I truly found my voice because of you.

To anybody reading this who has ever been involved in a prison ministry, thank you. The people who came faithfully every week to run classes with us became pillars in my life. They became mentors and like family. **Ms. Marci,** you are Jesus with skin on. I love you. **Ms. Laura, Ms. Bari, Ms. Becky, Ms. Debbie, Ms. Kim**—all of you mean so much to me. And sweet **Mr. Jim,** I hope you're up there singing, "Didn't I Walk on the Water."

To my Whitworth girls: **Alicia, Mama "Z," Erin, Ruth, Ashlea, Ms. Rice, April, Trina, Megan, Tia, Naomi,** and so many others. I learned how to be a friend because you ladies first showed me how.

Mark Cooley: Thank you for your contribution to this book and for flying my mom out to see me while I was in prison—those visitations meant everything. Thank you for having the most generous spirit of anybody I've ever known. Thank you for loving my family like you do.

Mike Aspland: Thank you for adopting me as your fourth daughter. Thank you for always being embarrassing, forcing me to go to school, making me cry, and ultimately giving me the greatest gift I could ever do for myself professionally. Thank you for bridging the gap between survivors and law enforcement. God used you to break down that wall for me. Thank you for being obedient to His call and for founding Set Free Monterey Bay.

To the **SFMB team:** Thank you for trusting me, for giving me a place to land, and for fighting for all the girls out there just like me.

To the **Jones Day team:** Jacqueline, Jeff, and Preston, thank you for helping me achieve another level of freedom.

KH: I know when we first met, I was supposed to be the one mentoring you, yet you have taught me so much. You are a mirror, reflecting back parts of myself. It has been one of the most rewarding experiences of my life to see you grow and heal. Thank you for allowing me to be a part of your rising.

Bonnie: I cannot thank you enough for your guidance. Thank you for always channeling my power back to me, for encouraging me to go within, to drop in and find the answer. Since I met you, I have evolved and transformed a few times over. It is because of who you are that I stand here embodied, self-assured, and continuously healing. You are one wise woman, with a character of gold liquid light.

Molly: God knows what we need, exactly when we need it. I just thank you for showing up when you did. You are my sister—my family. Thank you for loving me at every stage of my healing. Thank you for enriching my life with your incredible intellect, Tilly barks, and an endless supply of baked goods. Never have I felt more at home. I love you more than frosting.

Lexi and Lauren: Thank you for building this book into exactly what I had envisioned. Thank you for patiently dealing with my indecisiveness. Thank you for your gentle nudges while editing, being cool with a couple of "F-bombs," and making this book into its final version. Lex, I appreciate all your detail-oriented "oneness." Who knew we would be doing this twenty years later?

J: For Morgan Wallen and lavender lattes.

Bhalo: My handsome boy. I know the story goes that I rescued you, but thank you for flying all the way from Korea to rescue me.

To my **papa,** who wanted nothing more than for me to write a book. I can imagine your hand on my shoulder as you say, "Good work, babe."

Jesus: What You did for me on the cross was enough, yet You continue to fill my cup again and again. Thank You for redeeming my life from the pit. Thank You for the healing. Thank You for making me into the woman I am today. All I want to do is what You want me to. I hope You are proud of me.

Finally, to **my readers**, I am grateful for every single one of you. The book you hold in your hands is a dream God placed on the inside of me, and when I finally sat down to write, it came pouring out. Whether you are a friend or a stranger, I pray this book made an impact. Whether you are an expert on human trafficking or this is new to you, I am thankful for your curiosity and your search to understand more. We are not at fault for what we don't know—but once we know, what are we going to do about it? You *can* make a difference. Even if it is just one person, it is worth it.

BIBLIOGRAPHY

Grillo, Harmony (Dust). "Should Prostitution Be Decriminalized?" Treasures. Accessed Nov. 26, 2021. https://www.iamatreasure. com/blog/should-prostitution-be-legal.

Healthline. "Everything You Need to Know About DMT, the 'Spirit Molecule.'" Accessed Nov. 27, 2021. https://www.healthline.com/ health/what-is-dmt.

LePera, Nicole. *How to Do the Work: Recognize Your Patterns, Heal from Your Past, and Create.* New York: Harper Wave, 2021.

Stevens, Becca. *Love Heals.* Nashville: Thomas Nelson, 2017.

Van der Kolk, Bessel. *The Body Keeps the Score: Brain, Mind, and Body in the Healing of Trauma.* New York: Penguin Publishing Group, 2015.

ABOUT
SET FREE MONTEREY BAY

Set Free Monterey Bay is a Christian organization established to help adult female (ages 18 and over) sex trafficking survivors find healing in a Christ-centered restoration home and to educate the Monterey Bay community about human trafficking.

For more information on Set Free Monterey Bay, please visit:

www.setfreemontereybay.org

Q&A WITH ASHLEY

In your opinion, what is the number one thing a woman caught in the web of sex trafficking needs to know?

That she is worthy of a new life and that it is accessible to her.

I think many victims are conditioned to believe that there isn't a way out. They are riddled with fear at the thought of leaving, and they begin to accept "the life" as their fate. This is a lie. There are ways to exit, and there is also so much more than what she is currently experiencing. Just by taking one foot and placing it outside "the life," so much can begin to shift for her.

What are some preventative measures parents and mentors can take to help keep girls off the streets?

What is happening now looks very different than when I was being trafficked. Even as a contemporary survivor-leader, I learn new things every day about how "the game" now operates. Online safety would be my number one priority when parenting or mentoring a young person today. Not to instill fear in them, but to help them play defense against recruiters and predators.

Traffickers are not dumb—they are master manipulators. I see this today with other survivors I have helped. The minute a trafficker realizes you are out of their grasp, they want that control back. They will say anything to get you back in their game. They begin trying to woo you and manipulate you into thinking you need them. Of course, this is a lie, and as those tactics fail, the contact can become more aggressive and turn violent.

We need to instill in our young women the truth that they do not need to seek validation through a screen, boys, or men. That they hold intrinsic value in just being who they are. I wish I had known that as a teen. I think my family and mentors tried everything they could, but I just didn't realize my value.

When I was being trafficked, I didn't know about human trafficking. Language is so important, and today we have language to put with this topic and what is happening to people. In my case, since I didn't have the words, I fed an addiction, which was a powerful thing—more powerful than my family or anybody else who cared about me. As residual effects from abuse lay dormant inside me, I just kept running, and those around me eventually watched me burn my life to the ground—until Jesus made beauty from the very thing I had burned down.

The book talks a lot about trauma and people's responses to trauma. What are some of the key things parents and mentors can do to help women heal so they can change their lives?

Parents and mentors need to understand that healing is never linear, and they need to be patient with the *process*.

Be prepared for setbacks and even relapses. Accept these things as part of the process—a not-so-fun part but a necessary one for many survivors. It's important for parents and mentors to know that a setback is not a reflection on them or what they did or didn't do.

You may need to do a deep dive into this topic and educate yourself on the effects of trauma. This can prove helpful in not taking responsibility for the actions and responses of the survivor you are walking with.

Also, I cannot stress therapy enough. I don't mean sticking the woman in a square box talking to just anybody—but finding somebody who understands trauma, a person the survivor clicks with. This may take *many* tries, but eventually she'll find the right person.

Trusting a therapist—a good therapist—has propelled me forward in my healing journey. Help this woman find what works for her and help her pursue it, letting her have autonomy over who that person is and what style of therapy is being presented (EMDR, IFS, equine, etc.).

What's the most important thing to keep in mind when ministering to a woman in this situation?

That *we* are not anybody's rescuer.

You may minister to a woman, advocate for her, or simply just have a conversation—yet Jesus is the One who rescues. Your words and actions may fall on deaf ears the first, second, or even tenth time you talk to somebody in the life of exploitation. However, know you planted a seed. I can recall many words that were spoken to me when I wasn't ready to receive them, yet they all played a part in leading me to my freedom—leading me to Jesus and *His* rescue.

TAKE ACTION

WHAT YOU CAN DO TO FIGHT AGAINST DOMESTIC SEX TRAFFICKING

- Spread awareness. Share this book. Talk to your friends, family, and children about the issue. Join the anti-trafficking movement and stand up for the cause. Survivors need YOU.

- Learn more about sex trafficking. Educate yourself.

- Call the National Human Trafficking Hotline if you see something suspicious. Here is their number: 888-373-7888.

- Connect with organizations in your local community that are fighting against sex trafficking. (For example, Set Free Monterey Bay.)

- Contact your local middle and high schools to make sure they are educating children about trafficking.

- Contact service providers and local police in your area, and find out how you can help fight against sex trafficking.

- Donate to Set Free Monterey Bay or other organizations/ programs dedicated to helping survivors succeed. For more information on Set Free Monterey Bay, visit www. setfreemontereybay.org.